Collective Intelligence

How to build a business that's smarter than you

Jennifer Sundberg & Pippa Begg

Published by
LID Publishing
An imprint of LID Business Media Ltd.
LABS House, 15-19 Bloomsbury Way,
London, WC1A 2TH, UK

info@lidpublishing.com
www.lidpublishing.com

A member of:

BPR⊛

businesspublishersroundtable.com

Printed by Gutenberg Press, Malta
ISBN: 978-1-911687-92-4
ISBN: 978-1-911687-93-1 (ebook)

Cover design: Tim Brook
Page design: Caroline Li

Collective Intelligence

How to build a business that's smarter than you

Jennifer Sundberg & Pippa Begg

MADRID | MEXICO CITY | LONDON
BUENOS AIRES | BOGOTA | SHANGHAI

Contents

What's this book about and why should you read it?

This book for leaders isn't about leaders, leading or even leadership. It won't make you smarter, because you're already smart. You don't need that.

This book is about how you can get *everyone* in your business to think better – not by doing the thinking for them, but by equipping them with the right tools and helping them form new habits. It's about building a collective intelligence that is greater than the sum of its intellectual parts, including yours.

Why? Because brains are why we employ humans and not robots, and we're wasting an awful lot of brainpower by not using them. As long as there is thinking that only humans can and should do, it's down to leaders like you to help them do it better.

Collective intelligence – building a business that's smarter than its CEO – is what powers the most enduringly successful businesses. It helps businesses to conquer the world and is the secret to staying nimble at scale. In this book we'll show you why it works and how to do it.

We can do that because we've seen inside businesses in a way that others haven't, and we've seen how smart businesses get built.

Where the work of most consultants stops at the boardroom door, the nature of our work at Board Intelligence over the past 15 years has put us squarely in the room. In the furnace of the world's most demanding boardrooms, we developed a playbook for helping leaders, from Fortune 500s to government departments, to make smarter, faster decisions.

Over time, we realised those board-level decisions were the tip of the iceberg. That for every decision made in the boardroom, many more were taken outside of it. All the more so in the most successful businesses, where the centre of gravity for decision-making was much closer to the front line. And where everyone – from the boardroom to the shop floor – was given the tools, skills, and confidence to use their brains and take decisions.

Since then, it's been our mission to help our clients (3,000 and counting) to tap into their collective intelligence, giving them the playbook to unleash the combined thinking power of their people at every level.

This book is our attempt to share what we've learned along the way, so others can do it too. We'll show you how badly run businesses make smart people act dumb and take you inside companies that are systematically designed for everyone to think well.

Most importantly, we'll show you how to move from the first group to the second, transforming how your business thinks, communicates, and gets things done by creating the conditions for people to use their brains and apply them where it matters most.

And yes, that part will require some leadership. Get it right, and it may well be the smartest thing you ever did.

Upside-down

How do you grow big and stay nimble?

"Why am I here?"

It wasn't as glamorous as I (Jen) had imagined it would be.

In the movies, the boardroom of a multibillion-dollar company like this one would be perched at the top of a skyscraper, looking down through huge windows on the city and the ant-like people below. A huge table, so shiny with polish you could see your reflection in it, would fill the room.

This room had no particular outlook, just the dirty grey stone of the buildings opposite. But as the directors filed in, in their sharply tailored suits, it felt like a seat of power – a room in which hugely important decisions would be thrashed out by hotshot business leaders at the top of their game.

To this day, it's hard to explain why I was there. I wasn't a member of the board, but a consultant who'd been working with the CEO for a few months. I think he was trying to be helpful, exposing me to the inner workings of a big company boardroom to help my career. He was right; a few months later I'd meet my future business partner Pippa and together we'd pivot my consultancy business to tackle what I saw that day.

But for now, I took my seat at the table and watched, grateful for the opportunity to observe what really went on in rooms like this one. The chair, a tall man with broad shoulders, called the room to order and the meeting began. At the table was a Cambridge University technology professor who advised the British government. Sat beside him was a former ambassador, an American high-growth guru, and a handful of British industrialists. Then there were the senior executives and me.

The business had just missed out on a mega-deal and everyone around that table knew it was going to hurt. The loss had opened up a gaping hole in their plans which needed to be filled urgently. The problem was that their core market was showing the early signs of decline and it wasn't obvious where this much-needed revenue would come from. The board needed to make its next move. And fast.

This was the stuff business school case studies were made of, and I was eager to see what the board would come up with. But, as the minutes ticked by, it became clear that I wouldn't find out that day. Because over the next four hours, nothing much happened.

The directors turned over the first page of the stack of papers in front of them – a great brick of a document, packed full of presentations and reports with every imaginable cut of operational performance data – and worked their way through it.

The big gnarly issue went untouched. As the meeting drew to a close, nobody was any the wiser as to how to solve it. And their next chance to discuss it would be at the next board meeting, scheduled for a month's time.

Later that day, as we took a cab to another meeting, the CEO gave me a frank assessment of the board meeting I'd just observed. "I've been a board member for two decades now and I've seen the same thing happen time and again. You take a group of intelligent, strategic thinkers with bucket loads of highly relevant experience, plonk them in a room together and then watch as something goes horribly wrong."

Over the next few months, the business's share price would tumble and the company would shed 50% of its workforce. A 150-year-old business would find itself in terminal decline, eventually being broken up and sold off in parts.

While there's no doubt this caused pain to everyone involved, businesses go bust all the time. At the time, the financial crisis was gathering steam and big businesses were going to the wall every day. So why does this business's demise play such a significant role in our story?

Because it got me thinking about why it happens and the role boards play in it.

I had some sympathy for the growing argument that boards were to blame. At the time, the stories coming out of the banks suggested directors were either asleep at the wheel or just plain bad.

But, having met this particular board, I knew it wasn't that simple. These weren't inept, uncaring or evil people. Were boards being set up to fail?

In any other walk of life, we take our superstars and enable them to the hilt. The best racing drivers get the best cars. The best jockeys get the best horses. In contrast, these directors were locked in a dingy room for four hours once a month and expected to see what no one else could.

I didn't know what tools they needed, but I was motivated to find out.

———————

Across town, I (Pippa) had just quit my job. After a few years working at HM Treasury and in asset management, I'd been tempted into the glamorous world of hedge funds. With an office overlooking the twinkling lights of Sloane Square and dinners at Annabel's, I was looking forward to the cut and thrust of a high-octane business.

It didn't take long for the sheen to come off. All around me were the signs of poisonous, out of control, hubris and a dangerous lack of governance and controls. It drove behaviour that I couldn't stand and saw no hope of fixing.

So I did the only thing I could, and quit. Disenchanted with the world of finance, I spotted an advert Jen had posted on our old university's careers board and went to meet her.

As Jen described her experience of the boardroom to me, it sounded familiar. An unusual quirk of my time in asset management was that, by my mid-20s, I'd sat in more than my fair share of board meetings, having attended the quarterly board meetings of the funds we managed. I'd witnessed the same problem there. Groups of smart, experienced, sensible people who seemed unable to get stuck in when they really needed to. And yet, coming out of that hedge fund, I now knew better than anyone the dangers of unchecked power and weak governance.

Fixing these problems felt important to both of us. So we decided to team up to try and tackle them.

Over the next few years, thanks to a lot of trial and error, we developed a playbook to help boards have better conversations and make faster decisions about the things that matter. We called it the Question Driven Insight Principle, or QDI Principle for short. We built a successful business around it, earning a nickname, 'the board whisperers,' and a client roster we were proud of.

It might come as a surprise then, to find out that this book isn't about how to run a great board meeting or why great boards unlock organizational performance. In fact, it's not about the board at all.

"I don't need a better board"

We've emerged from this experience as cheerleaders, not for boardroom intelligence, but for *collective* intelligence. What we learned was that to be successful, businesses need to think well and act fast at *every* level. To move quickly, to leapfrog the competition, you need your whole organization to have better conversations about the things that matter, not just the board.

Why?

Time and again, we felt we'd 'fixed' the board problem – the conversations were more focused, the information more insightful, the directors happier that they were adding more value. But it wasn't enough. Boards were working at full pelt but they were still slowing their organizations down. There were just too many decisions for them to make. A director once complained to us that his board needed a horizontal agenda to deal with its 20 'number one' priorities.

With such a vast remit that only ever seemed to expand, they had no hope of catching up. The board was a major bottleneck.

This wasn't something you could fix by adding more board meetings to the calendar, or creating more committees. These businesses needed fewer decisions flowing to the board full stop.

The lightbulb moment came when we met Sir John Timpson, chairman and owner of the eponymous UK shoe repair chain. A larger-than-life character with a broad grin and white hair, his business was a major name on the UK high street and he was a high-profile leader.

We'd been invited to pitch to him, and we went in with what we thought was a compelling message: let us help you get more value from your board.

He was kind enough to let us get five slides in before he cut to the chase. "I don't need a better board," he said. "The important decisions in this business aren't made in our boardroom."

It turns out that he was a fervent believer in 'upside-down management' – inverting the hierarchy and putting decision-making power into the hands of those on the shop floor.

As he later told us: "I don't like being told what to do, so there's no reason why anyone else should. Our store staff understand our customers the best, so we've put them in charge. Management is there to support and empower our staff and this rolls up to the board."[1]

In this upside-down hierarchy, the role of management was not to control customer-facing colleagues but to help them.

"What [upside-down management] does for our employees is transform their lives by giving them greater control of how they run their own work affairs," Timpson later explained to *HR Magazine*.[2] And the results speak for themselves. The 150-year-old business regularly wins 'best place to work' and customer service awards, enjoys high staff retention rates, and has grown to over 2,000 stores while the high street has waged its battle with online retail.[3]

In one sentence, Timpson challenged everything we thought we knew about how companies worked and set us on a new path. From that point onwards, we could see the problem and the opportunity more clearly. Fix the board and you'll only get so far. Get the whole business thinking well and making smart decisions and you don't just fix the bottleneck problem – you tap into the insight, experience and intelligence of everyone in the business, helping it go further, faster.

Move fast and ~~break~~ make things

These weren't just the musings of a maverick contrarian who got lucky. Since meeting Timpson, we've discovered that a similar philosophy drives some of the world's most enduringly successful businesses – including many run by superstar CEOs you wouldn't expect to be fans, let alone flagbearers, for running businesses this way.

Take Amazon, for example. A few years ago, we were in the early stages of developing a new software product and got in touch with a former colleague who'd gone on to work at the ecommerce giant. We were hunting for insights that would help us build and successfully launch a technology product. But what we got was a lesson in collective intelligence.

> "At Amazon we spend a lot of time writing documents, because it helps you think things through and gives others confidence that you've done so. That builds trust, which helps us move quickly – you don't have to go up the chain on every decision. Deep thinking is a hugely important part of Amazon's entrepreneurialism."

This was news to us. The popular narrative would suggest their success is all about finding a genius CEO, and then getting out of their way so they can move fast and break things.

But the reality is altogether different, not just at Amazon, but at businesses like Berkshire Hathaway, Apple, Microsoft and Salesforce too.

Steve Jobs didn't invent the iPhone. In fact, he wasn't keen on the mobile market at all.[4] Thankfully some of his colleagues saw it differently.[5]

And if it had been down to Warren Buffett, one of the world's most famous superstar CEOs, his investment firm Berkshire Hathaway would never have bought Apple stocks. One of his recently-hired lieutenants placed the bet, and it has paid off handsomely for the firm, making it their largest and most successful investment to date.[6]

The most successful CEOs don't hoard power, they see their role as helping others to think well so they can delegate decision making with confidence. And their businesses value slow, deep thinking and rigorous decision making. They know that putting the hard yards in early on helps them move faster in the long run, because they make fewer missteps along the way.

Nobody knows this better than Ann Hiatt, former executive assistant to Jeff Bezos at Amazon and later chief of staff to Marissa Meyer and then Eric Schmidt at Google. After meeting her at a conference where we were both speaking on a panel, I (Jen) couldn't help but ask if what we'd heard was really true. "I think these larger-than-life CEOs are misunderstood when you only see the glorified *Fortune* cover version of them," she told me. "For sure, their confidence and vision are incomparable.

But they also think hard about how to help others to think well. And unquestionably that is why they have been as successful as they are."

She cited Amazon Prime, the brainchild of a relatively junior engineer, as a perfect example of this in action. "It all came from just a regular employee saying, 'I think we're only serving half of our users with our current offering. What about the people who have more money than time?' That question put us on the path to developing the membership model we now know as Prime, and fulfilling Amazon's 'everything store' vision."

Collective intelligence

So, it turns out that the best companies systematically empower everyone (not just the CEO) to think well, and are set up to convert that intelligence into action faster than most companies.

This is what we mean by collective intelligence.

It means everyone is using their brains – rigorously and consistently – and acting on the insights that they generate. Because they don't have to keep coming back to senior management, people are able to make decisions with greater speed and closer to the problem, removing those frustrating bottlenecks. Because they make use of everyone's minds, they produce better thinking and make better decisions.

It may be what underpins the famed agility of tech businesses like Apple and Amazon, but it's not just limited to Silicon Valley. From high street retailers like Timpson to mining companies and banks, any business can learn its lessons.

It's been our mission for over a decade to apply and refine these lessons, developing our Question Driven Insight playbook not just in the living laboratory of our own business but with our clients too – businesses with superstar CEOs who turned out to be wrecking balls, consumer services firms derailed by mis-selling scandals, lumbering giants who just wanted to be more nimble.

What we've learned boils down to two things.

First, intelligence is an applied capability and you can create the conditions to help it flourish. As Charles Darwin – a man who, it's reported, occupied the middle of the IQ distribution curve – put it, "Even people who aren't geniuses can outthink the rest of mankind if they develop certain thinking habits."

We first witnessed this in the boardroom 15 years ago and have since seen it play out at every level of management across every industry. You can't just throw smart people in a room together and expect them to make magic. But, just as the wrong conditions can stultify smart people, it is also possible to enhance everyone's ability to apply their minds if you can create the right conditions.

Doing so means you can make every decision – big and small – smarter and faster. And the more we practise good thinking, the better we get at it. It's like going to the gym; if we exercise our brains every day, we can eventually take in our stride the things that used to leave us gasping.

Second, you can create the conditions for collective intelligence by equipping everyone in the business with three capabilities: critical thinking, great communication, and a focus on the problems and opportunities that matter most.

Because, without critical thinking, we're starved of the insights and ideas that will take us further, faster. Without great communication, those ideas and insights go nowhere because we can't rally others behind them and compel them to action. If we don't focus all this on a shared view of what matters most, we become busy fools, pulling in different directions.

Creating the conditions for collective intelligence is the smartest thing a leader can do. We need others to help us make sense of our complex, changing, uncertain and ambiguous world, and to meet its challenges with creativity and judgement. We need them to challenge us, so we don't fly too close to the sun. And it simply doesn't work to throw good thinkers at problems and hope for the best.

In this book we'll show you how to put those three elements into action: great thinking, clear communication and focus. We'll show you how it's done in Silicon Valley and elsewhere too, from our own scale up technology business to airlines and energy companies. Because every company has the potential to build and benefit from collective intelligence – yours included.

We'll start in Part 1 by showing you how to get everyone in your business doing their best thinking, with a little help from some dehydrated footballers.

Part I

Thinking

How will Part I help you build collective intelligence?

To build collective intelligence we all need to get better at asking questions, the sort that fuel curiosity and critical thinking. In Part I we'll show you how. It all comes down to rituals and rubber ducks.

─────── BOTTOM LINE UP FRONT ───────

Chapter 1

Spark and fuel

How do you get everyone thinking?

Game time

Something strange was happening in Gainesville, Florida in the summer of 1965. Every week Dewayne Douglas would stand in front of a crowd of baying onlookers who'd gathered to watch a group of beefy men shrink. We mean this literally: after a couple of hours, some of the men were 18lbs lighter than they were when they arrived.

It wasn't some new spectator dieting fad. The men were college football players at the University of Florida – the Florida Gators – battling it out with rival teams. And Douglas was their assistant coach, a former Gator whose professional playing career had been cut short by injury. When he wasn't coaching, he worked as a security officer at the university's health centre.

One day, after four cups of coffee and as many trips to the restroom, a question struck him as he chewed over their most recent game: Why aren't the players urinating more?

He recalled his own experiences as a player on the field – sweating, shrinking, losing weight and never feeling the need to urinate, no matter how much he drank. He wondered why.

It would have been easy to bat this question away. It was obvious, surely, why players didn't urinate during games – they were sweating so much they had no fluid left.

But Douglas didn't bat it away, and he put the question to his friend at the health centre, kidney specialist Dr Robert Cade, over another coffee. Douglas knew that urination was an important bodily function – expelling waste as well as excess fluid. So why would it grind to a halt on the football field? Surely, in the space of a few hours, at least some of the 30 players would feel the urge. It got the two of them talking and Cade thinking. He mused on whether there might be a connection with another phenomenon accepted as just one of those things, that player performance tails off dramatically during games. He decided to experiment.[1]

With careful analysis, Cade and his team of researchers discovered that, as well as losing water, players were losing electrolytes. This was upsetting the body's chemical balance and sending the kidneys into over drive trying to conserve water and salt in a battle to maintain blood volume.[2]

All this meant no urination and performances that diminished rapidly as games wore on, not to mention heat stroke and hospitalization when temperatures were high (as they often were in Gainesville).

Of course, the solution wasn't as simple as drinking more. Drinking water made players sluggish and prone to cramp by further diluting electrolytes, and sugary drinks did nothing to replenish salts. So, Cade challenged himself to find an alternative – one that would replace what the body was losing and keep the Gators going for longer.

His first few attempts fell flat. Nobody could stomach his foul-tasting concoction of glucose, sodium and phosphate until Cade's wife suggested adding lemon to mask the flavour. Four dozen lemons later, Cade finally had something he could test.[3]

It worked a treat, powering the freshmen to a miraculous second-half turnaround in their annual 'Toilet Bowl' game with the Gators B team. The varsity team's coach got wind and ordered a supply for the following day's much-anticipated game with Louisiana State. Cade leapt at the opportunity, borrowing glucose supplies from other labs in the medical school and cleaning out three local grocery stores' lemon supplies to produce 100 litres of the experimental drink.

The rest, as they say, is history. The electrolyte drink proved so effective that the Gators used it in every game for the rest of the season, and then started using it in practice too. Before long it was given a name, Gatorade, in honour of the football team. It went on to become a hugely successful business, now with $6bn sales in the US alone, and kick-started the sports drink sector.[4]

The story of Gatorade contains all the ingredients of critical thinking. Douglas and Cade's curiosity set off a chain reaction of questions, sparking insights that provided a practical basis for action. Ideas were tested and developed rigorously. Every failure brought the solution nearer. And there wasn't a CEO or Nobel prize-winning scientist in sight.

Millions of people had been watching the same American football games for decades. Hundreds of thousands will have known first-hand that locker room toilets went strangely unvisited during half-time breaks. Tens of thousands had the scientific knowledge to figure it out.

So why didn't any of them ask the questions that made all the difference? Why did Douglas and Cade?

We don't need
no education

Questions are the catalyst of intelligence, collective or otherwise. They stimulate our curiosity and creativity, and trigger critical thinking, surfacing insights and ideas that help us solve problems in new and useful ways.

We all start off as prodigious questioners. Research by Harvard shows that children bombard their caregivers with up to 100 questions a day between the ages of two and five, as they try to make sense of the world around them.[5]

But as we get older, something strange happens. As we learn more, we ask less. And by the age of 11 most children have stopped asking questions. Our innate curiosity withers away – and as parents, teachers and employers we are all fully complicit in it.

"There is what I call an answer orientation that permeates education, professional life and society at large," explains Dr Lani Watson, a research fellow at the University of Oxford whose work focuses on questions and questioning.

Formal education hones our ability to memorize answers, be they simple facts or more sophisticated explanations. Teachers ask children questions – not the other way around – and then reward them for giving the answer they (and the examiner) expect.

Because we're habituated from an early age to value answers, we start to lose the skill of asking good questions. "I've done a lot of work with schools, and I've not met a single teacher who disagrees with the idea that children start off asking questions, go through formal education, and then come out answering them," Watson explains.

An experience recounted in the book *The Hungry Mind* highlights just how back to front this is. In one 9th-grade art lesson, a student raised her hand to ask if there were any places in the world where no one made art. The teacher's response? "Zoe, no questions now, please; it's time for learning."[6]

This continues into adult life. At work, we expect people to show expertise in their area of specialization – to have answers. But by losing their questioning skill, they sacrifice their capacity for original, creative thought.

A test developed in the 1960s by psychologists Dr George Land and Dr Beth Jarman showed this in action. They asked a group of NASA job applicants and a group of 5-year-olds to identify as many different uses for a paperclip as possible. The children wiped the floor with the adults, embracing the power of "what if?" and coming up with all manner of ideas, from a tightrope for ants to a hula hoop for fairies. 98% of them scored at "genius level". In stark contrast, only 2% of the adults achieved this score. Most of them couldn't see past using paperclips to bind papers together.[7]

The decline and fall of photography giant Eastman Kodak shows what dire consequences can follow from this inertia of the imagination. One day in 1975, a group of executives gathered to hear a pitch from one of their employees, an excited young electrical engineer called Steve Sasson. He had with him a device about the size of a toaster – the world's first self-contained, digital camera.[8]

He started talking about its technical specifications and all the ways that it could be further improved. But the executives soon stopped him. The new camera was too clunky, one of them said. What was the point in releasing a product that would cannibalize their thriving photo film business, another asked. "That's cute," he said, paperclipping Sasson's blueprints together and filing them away, "but don't tell anyone about it."

Kodak was in the midst of a golden age, growing tenfold between 1962 and 1981. Its executives solved the problems that they thought needed solving – making quarterly numbers, incrementally improving products, optimizing supply chain and logistics, engaging their customers.

But had they asked, "What will eventually replace camera film, as camera film once replaced photographic plates?" or "If we don't sell digital cameras, who will?", then they would have seen a different set of problems. They might have seen an opportunity. And they might not have shelved Sasson's prototype so swiftly.

Forty years later, Satya Nadella spotted a similar problem taking root at Microsoft, where he was preparing to step up to the CEO role.

For all its past successes, Microsoft was losing ground. "The tech giant hadn't had a breakthrough innovation in decades," reported Stanford University's Behnam Tabrizi in *Harvard Business Review*.[9]

To Nadella, the root cause was clear: "Our culture had been rigid. Each employee had to prove to everyone that he or she knew it all and was the smartest person in the room". As a result, the business was being held back by internal power plays and a 'not invented here' mentality, and Microsoft increasingly found itself watching from the sidelines as its competitors made huge strides forward.[10]

Nadella had inherited what he called a 'know it all' culture. To get Microsoft back into the game, he needed to build a 'learn it all' culture and turn a company of world-class experts into a company of world-class questioners.

Getting back on the bike

Some people never lose their inquisitiveness and open-mindedness. The late Stephen Hawking once said, "I am just a child who has never grown up. I still keep asking these 'how' and 'why' questions. Occasionally, I find an answer."

But that doesn't mean the rest of us are doomed to be mindless automatons. Just as we learned to give good answers, so can we relearn how to ask good questions. We can get our questioning mojo back.

There are parallels with literacy. "If we were to go 400 years into the past ... about 15% of the population knew how to read," says educator Sal Khan.[11] "And I suspect that if you asked someone who did know how to read, 'what percentage of the population do you think is even capable of reading?' they might guess 20 or 30%. Today, we know that close to 100% of the population can read."

Giving people access to the necessary education and tools changed perceptions of human potential – and opened up a world of new opportunities.

If we apply the same logic to questioning – something we all started our lives knowing how to do – it no longer feels like a superpower for the precious few. It feels like something that's well within us all.

What if we gave everyone the right tools to ask more and better questions? Perhaps 98% of adults could score as highly in the paperclip test as those 5-year-olds. Perhaps one of your employees could imagine the next big thing, and not get shut down. By helping people rebuild the muscles that atrophied during their education, the remarkable could become the norm.

It's not a miracle cure: asking the right questions doesn't necessarily mean people will find the right answers. But, by equipping as many people as possible with the power of questions, we give ourselves a fighting chance.

So let's find out how.

Chapter 2

Questions

What makes a power question?

Too clever by half

CEOs are used to being in the spotlight and thinking on their feet, but this was different. As Rob Whiteman made his way through the rabbit warren of corridors in the Houses of Parliament and found the Select Committee hearing room, it felt like he was walking into a courtroom – and he was the one in the dock. He recalls the heat of the cameras and the sweat beading on his back as he took his seat in front of the panel of MPs.

In 2011, as the new head of the UK Border Agency,[1] he'd inherited a £2bn budget, 25,000 staff and a huge backlog of immigration cases which would take four decades to clear at their current rate of progress.[2]

Spears were flying at the Border Agency from all angles. Immigration was a political hot potato and never off the front pages, with the media feasting on stories of 'tidal waves' and a country 'overrun' by foreigners.[3]

There had been uproar the previous year when coach passengers were found to have been waved through without proper checks at the busy port of Dover – despite it being one of the main routes for illegal entry to the country.[4] And not long after Whiteman had joined the agency, an undercover journalist outed a corrupt immigration officer within its ranks, which only fanned the flames.[5]

Whiteman, an opera singer in his spare time, knew how to work an audience. Earlier in his career as a civil servant, he had been asked to appease an increasingly restless crowd that had gathered in a packed hall waiting for the results of an election count. He serenaded them with arias and after 20 minutes he had everyone, from politicians to vote counters, on their feet and clapping.

But today his role was an altogether different one. Whiteman sat up straight, organized his papers and took a deep breath. The chair gave him a clear instruction – answer the questions directly and don't waste the MPs' time – and then the questions started flying.

In all he was grilled for over three hours by the committee, in what felt more like an inquisition than an inquiry. "They had prepared over 60 closed and care fully worded questions for me, each one intended to uncover more backlogs and reveal new problems. They went through them methodically and at speed. They had to, or they wouldn't get through them all," Whiteman recalls.

He felt like the proverbial swan – struggling to appear calm, feathers unruffled, while guarding every word leaving his dry throat for fear of it being twisted and turned against him.

And, as the questions rained down on him, he realized how long his inquisitors must have spent agitating over them. "They were each desperate to be the one to deliver the killer blow," he said.

———————

Years later, Whiteman became a client of ours and he shared this story as we explored our mutual fascination with the power of good questions.

Looking back, it was clear to Whiteman how utterly ineffective the MPs' over-engineered questions were, leading them down rabbit hole after rabbit hole. And he wondered if they might have achieved more if they'd taken a different approach. "What they never asked me was 'What's going on? What concerns you?', which would have given them so much more. If they'd asked me what was wrong, I was duty-bound to tell them."

Clever questions are great for debate winning and point scoring. They can be used to establish status (*"I'm* the one asking the questions around here") or catch people out ("So when did you stop shoplifting?").

But what we've learned is that if you use questions like weapons, that's all they'll be. And if you're looking for questions as tools for better thinking, stop trying to be so clever. Overly complex questions are almost never as useful as the most straightforward and obvious ones. The ones that are often so obvious that we neglect to ask them, either because we assume we already know the answer or because we don't want to look stupid by admitting we don't. The ones that, if we don't ask them, can leave us with dangerous blind spots or judgements built on flawed foundations, like "What happened?" or "Why?" or "So what?"

We spent years asking our clients what questions were on their minds and helping them to work out which drove the most insight. The conclusion we came to in our search for great questions is that the best questions are the simplest ones.

What we need is to learn how and when to use them, to adapt them to our given context. In other words, we need to learn how to become better *questioners*.

Lessons from master questioners

In 1989, a pair of Californian slackers travelled back in time to find historical figures to help with their high school presentation. Among these was the venerable philosopher Socrates (known to his bodacious new friends as "So-Craits"), who communicated his wisdom with them largely through over-the-top hand gestures. If you haven't seen the movie, Bill and Ted ace the assignment.[6]

They chose well – there has arguably been no better teacher than Socrates, whose disciples included Plato and Aristotle, who later tutored Alexander the Great. A shoeless subversive, unwashed, unkempt, pot-bellied, the very opposite of the Ancient Greek ideal of outward beauty reflecting inner virtue, Socrates changed Western thought forever, without directly bequeathing a great many truths or grand theories.

All he did, really, was ask questions. Lots of questions. Plato relayed tales of Socrates wandering the narrow, dusty streets and bustling agora of Athens in the 5th century BC, engaging the great and good in search of what things truly were, challenging everything, relentlessly probing, testing, clarifying – all for the sake of knowledge itself.

Socrates asked the poet to define poetry and the general to define courage and, with sure, deft, strokes exposed the flaws, faulty assumptions, gaps and contradictions in what they said. One wealthy man argued that justice was paying back what was due. "Is it just to return a borrowed sword to a friend who's gone insane?" Socrates replied, earnestly.

His co-conversationalists invariably left knowing considerably less than they had thought, and Socrates died jesting that he must be the wisest man in Greece because he alone knew that he knew nothing. In so doing, he showed us that it is in the asking – not the answering – that wisdom is really found.

He also showed us a few things about what great questioners do. First, they question everything. Socrates was driven by intense curiosity. He had a thirst to know, and nothing was off-limits, no matter how sacred or obvious.

No self-respecting Athenian had thought to ask what poetry was before. They quite reasonably assumed that they already knew, just as beverage industry executives had never thought to investigate how athletes' bathroom habits might present them with a billion-dollar business opportunity. But, because he questioned everything, Socrates was able to see through the assumptions and received wisdom that so easily go unquestioned, and to untangle the fallacies and what we would now call cognitive biases that we all suffer from.

The second key lesson to take from Socrates is that he never stopped asking questions. He was almost never satisfied with the first answer he heard. He kept digging and drilling down to first principles, which is the essence of critical thinking. And he showed that this is the only way to truly make sense of things as they are and, therefore, discern what to do next.

This is not some ivory tower exercise. The same principles of curiosity and critical thinking can be seen applied to great, practical effect in modern business.

Take Frank Gehry. Still going strong in his nineties, the Pritzker Architecture Prize-winning architect is renowned for feats of artistic vision married with ground-breaking engineering and his buildings grace some of the most expensive real estate in the world.

Not unrelatedly, he has a Socrates-esque knack of asking simple questions.

In 1991, he was invited by regional government officials to Bilbao, the largest city in Spain's Basque region. It's a beautiful part of the world, with lush green hills and a dramatic coastline. But the city itself had seen better days. "Bilbao was not quite as bad as Detroit, but almost," Gehry later recalled. "Steel industry gone. Shipping industry gone. It looked pretty sad."[7]

The officials wanted him to transform a former wine warehouse in a run-down corner of the city into a modern art gallery. They were excited to hear his pitch and were somewhat taken aback when Gehry's sketchbook remained unopened, in the bag by his feet, during the meeting. Instead, he asked a simple question: "Why are you doing this?"

This question had long acted as Gehry's creative launchpad. "I grew up in a Talmudic household, and the Talmud starts with the question 'Why?' It is a built-in formula for curiosity, and curiosity is the lifeblood of creativity," he once told the *Financial Times*.[8]

It took some digging, but eventually Gehry could put his finger on what his clients in Bilbao really wanted – and their ambitions were rather loftier than the original brief had implied. They wanted the building to do for their post-industrial city what the Opera House had done for Sydney – to change its image and put it on the map.

It quickly became clear that they needed a different approach to deliver this grand vision. Rather than renovate an old building which was poorly suited to modern art, Gehry suggested they construct a bold new building on a derelict but spectacular waterfront site.

It was an approach that the officials hadn't even realized they wanted, until Gehry had thoroughly probed their assumptions.

The Guggenheim Museum Bilbao, with its shimmering, fish-like titanium scales, is now world-famous. It was an architectural triumph, and the 'Bilbao effect' not only triggered a revival of the city's fortunes, it also inspired countless other urban regeneration projects around the globe. The building succeeded in "squaring up to both its context and the ambitious mandate of its client, while clearly sustaining a logic and life of its own," according to *Architecture Review*, which went on to claim that "the international art world has a new dot on its map and Bilbao has a new Atlantic star."[9]

Perhaps even more remarkable than the architecture was Gehry's management of the project. The building went up in four years, as forecast, and came in under its $100m budget, which, as anyone who's ever done an extension will know, is borderline miraculous.

In comparison, the Sydney Opera House came in nine years late and 15 times over budget. Under political pressure to show progress, the thinking and planning phase was rushed and construction kicked off with little more than the architect's "magnificent doodle" to guide it. Costs ballooned and parts of the building had to be blown up and rebuilt. And even when it was complete, the project was far from finished, with flawed acoustics and an air conditioning system that was so aggressive it would turn the pages of the orchestra's sheet music. All wholly unsuitable for a live music venue.

According to a University of Oxford analysis of 16,000 large-scale public works, only 0.5% deliver on time, on budget and also deliver the intended benefits.[10] The fact that Gehry's projects usually fall within that 0.5% is testament to the time saved by rigorous, and early, questioning.

How to help others get better at questioning

Curiosity and critical thinking are both driven by asking questions. But in the absence of one-on-one coaching from ancient Greek philosophers (or famous architects), how can you help people get better at asking them?

The first step is to make questioning easier, and the easiest way to do that is to give people somewhere to start.

Imagine you're on an American football field (again). Your opponents are arrayed in front of you, low and coiled, each player marked for collision in a high-velocity scramble for the ball that belies significant levels of tactical sophistication. There is no time to think (let alone take a bathroom break). You need a touchdown, and when the whistle blows, you need a plan of action to get the ball down the field.

What you turn to is a 'play,' a set piece developed with the help of your coach, memorized by all players, and deployed when the quarterback barks out a coded signal ("Green 19, Green 19, set hut!").

It's the same concept as learning a chess opening – a well-practised set of moves that acts as the foundation for subsequent thought, and that means you don't have to go back to first principles every time.

In business, we can use similarly rehearsed patterns of questions to tackle common situations – from setting plans to taking stock of our progress in delivering them. These patterns, which we've come to refer to as 'Question Driven Insight plays,' or 'QDI plays' for short, help to get you off to a strong start and make it easy for everyone to get with the programme.

Let's take a routine performance update, for example. We've read thousands of them, and they tend to read more like press releases than the full, frank updates they should be. They do a great job of showing just how busy the author has been, and a terrible job of sharing what's *really* keeping them awake at night and what needs to be done about it. They should, instead, be a place for sharing unvarnished news and surfacing ideas for continuous improvement or tactical pivots. And the way to achieve that is to boil it down to the five simple questions in this QDI play:

1. What are we trying to achieve?
2. What's gone well and what has not?
3. What are the key risks and opportunities?
4. Given all of this, what should we stop doing/ start doing/do differently?
5. Are we confident we'll achieve our aims?

If you're thinking these questions are far too simple to capture the complexity of your business, you may be surprised to learn that this QDI play has helped global banks and small charities alike to think critically about their performance and how best to move forward.

You can see a similarly simplistic approach in a wide variety of highly successful organizations. If you've served in the British Army since 2001, you'll be familiar with the Combat Estimate, a seven-question framework designed to help commanders rapidly formulate plans, even in the most difficult circumstances.[11] Whether you've found yourself on the wrong side of mortar fire, or needing to secure a bridgehead or escort a convoy, you'd ask:

1. What is the enemy doing and why?
2. What have I been told to do and why?
3. What actions/effects do I want to have on the enemy?
4. Where can I best accomplish each action/effect?
5. What resources do I need?
6. When and where do these actions take place?
7. What control measures do I need to impose?

The strength of the framework is its simplicity; it can be used at all levels in the chain of command, from section (eight soldiers) to division (20,000), to quickly ensure nothing is overlooked. As a result, it's been adopted by militaries all over the world and deployed in a wide range of business environments, from management consultancy to COVID-19 crisis response.

If your scene is more big tech than battlefield, you may be more familiar with Amazon's six-pagers and simulated press releases (known internally as PRFAQs), which are narrative memos that the company's executives craft when developing ideas and plans or reporting on projects and performance.

Documents like these have underpinned all of Amazon's most successful innovations, including their cloud services business Amazon Web Services (AWS). As ex-Amazonian and Doc Bar Raiser founder Charlotte Woffindin told us, "Before a single line of code was written, the team spent 18 months writing the AWS PRFAQ, honing what it was, why customers needed it and how it would work. Whilst to some this would have felt like wasted time, it meant when they started, they were clear what they were building and why."

Although approaches to the PRFAQ vary within Amazon, they broadly follow this pattern:

1. What problem are we trying to solve?
2. Who are we solving it for?
3. Is the problem one we should solve?
4. What is the solution?
5. What questions will our customers ask us?
6. What questions will our colleagues ask us?

These form, in essence, a question framework, much like the Combat Estimate or a QDI play for a performance review. The specific questions being asked in these different contexts vary widely, but the approach is common – by starting with the most obvious and important questions, everyone can organize their thinking and avoid leaving gaps.

From set plays to freestyling

Hold on a minute, says your inner Socrates. Giving people preloaded sets of obvious questions is all very well, but isn't the idea to unleash collective intelligence by getting them to ask their own questions? Doesn't this approach, in effect, attempt to do the thinking for them?

It may seem counterintuitive, but don't forget how easy it is to overlook the simple questions that drive the most insight. We need help to keep them front of mind.

It also gets around the dreaded 'blank sheet' problem. Questioning is an inherently creative task – your imagination is the only thing that limits what you can ask. But staring at an empty page notoriously stifles creativity, precisely because you could write anything.

As Albert Read, a former journalist and publisher of *British Vogue*, *Vanity Fair* and *Tatler*, wrote in *The Imagination Muscle*: "The imagination needs structure to thrive. Prehistoric paintings of animals follow the contours of the cave wall. Poetic skill comes from obeying or rebelling against time-honoured forms. Like a child making a papier mâché mask, the imagination requires a balloon around which it can drape its first tender ideas."[12]

Another way to think of the relationship between fixed questions and fluid questioning is improvised jazz. When jazz musicians come together to jam, they don't pluck strings or hit keys at random. They use rules and freedom, in perfect balance, to find the right note – playing to a rhythm and within keys, and using tried and tested techniques to guide their individual free-styling and blend it with others.

This combination of rules and freedom has been particularly potent for global sports powerhouse Nike, which has trained generations of its leaders to think critically.

To understand how, we spoke to a client, Silvana Bonello, who had spent 19 years with Nike rising from logistics specialist to international leadership roles. For Silvana and her peers, Nike's world-famous global leadership development programme – which equips people with set plays, while also giving them the skills and confidence to freestyle when they need to – was key.

"What it gave us was a framework within which we could be free – a suite of questions we could use, whether we were at our HQ in Oregon or a factory in Vietnam. It was like a toolset. And using it gave us the confidence to challenge the status quo and do it really fast," she recalls of her time in the scheme.

How to find the right questions

Whether you're devising a QDI play for lots of people to use, or freestyling for a one-off, it helps to map out the questions visually to understand how they relate to each other. This makes it easier to find and fill the gaps.

Former McKinsey consultant Barbara Minto shared ways of doing this in her 1973 classic, *The Pyramid Principle*. Our favourite is to approach it much like one would a family tree.

If ideas are *siblings*, then, like any good parent, you need to make sure you don't miss any out. When talking about the impact of a decision on stakeholders, second-level thinking would list all of your stakeholders, not just some. Similarly, when writing a SWOT analysis, you wouldn't list strengths, weaknesses and opportunities without also covering threats.

If ideas are *parents and children*, that is, following a logic flow where one thing leads to another, then you're looking for missed steps (or generations).

- **What is going wrong?**
  We are regularly running out of stock, hurting sales and customer relationships.
- **What is causing it?**
  We have outgrown our supplier's maximum capacity.
- **How material is it?**
  Several of our biggest contracts are at risk because of this. In total these contracts are worth 30% of our revenue.
- **What should we do?**
  We need to diversify our supply chain and find new suppliers.

If any one of these steps were missed, and you didn't explore why there was an issue, its likely impact or what you could do about it, you could reach the wrong decision or take no decision at all.

Knowing the ground rules of questioning – that you can challenge anything, that every answer can lead to another question, and every question can and should be broken down into simpler parts – and starting with the basics gives people the structure to use their imagination.

In time, they can develop the confidence not only to think more deeply and rigorously at pace than ever before, but also to go off-piste when they need to. In turn, this gives leaders confidence that people will address the basics and then go beyond, basing their insights, decisions and ideas on more solid foundations.

That's what should happen, at least. But you know the old saying about leading a horse to water.

To make questioning something that people just do, to a high level, all the time, you need to find a way of turning it into a habit and making it stick. It's just like giving up chocolate or committing to daily 6am gym sessions for your New Year's resolution.

How hard could it be?

Chapter 3

Rituals and rubber ducks

How do you turn questioning
into a daily habit?

Lifting the hood

Eiji couldn't help but feel overawed as he surveyed the towering chimneys, the endless chain of cathedral-like factories, and the crawling pipes, trucks, and workers that serviced them.

This wasn't just any American car plant, or any American car company. In 1950, Ford's River Rouge plant in Dearborn, Michigan was the largest and most complex manufacturing facility that had ever been built, anywhere. Ford itself was an emblem of mid-20th century US industrial might, a business that had shaken the Earth by pioneering assembly line mass production.

For Eiji Toyoda, coming from a nation still reeling from the Second World War, it was a humbling experience. Where his company, Toyota, made 40 cars a day, Ford made 8,000. As Eiji put it, "You might as well compare a pebble with a boulder."[1]

Years earlier, Eiji had joined his uncle's textile works fresh out of university. But Eiji and his older cousin Kiichiro had their own dream, and it didn't involve textiles. They wanted to make cars. Eiji's uncle, a prolific inventor, had agreed to give over a corner of his factory to setting up an automobile company, saying, "Everyone should tackle some great project at least once in their life. I devoted most of my life to inventing new kinds of looms. Now it is your turn. You should make an effort to complete something that will benefit society."

By 1950 Eiji and Kiichiro had outgrown their corner of the warehouse, moved to a new site nearby, and had rebadged from Toyoda to Toyota, the former needing 10 strokes to write in Japanese and the latter only eight – a lucky number. But despite taking charge of the omens, they had a long way to go to become world beaters. Looking for inspiration, Eiji convinced officials at Ford Motor Company to let him visit their manufacturing complex for three months, to watch and learn how it should be done.

As an inquisitive Eiji toured the facilities and chatted with Ford employees, awe quickly faded to disappointment. The American company was far from the model of efficiency and effectiveness that he'd expected.

Instead of a slick, high-tech production system he found himself back in the 1930s, surrounded by mountains of inventory, with defective components lying undiscovered for weeks and workers toiling away to add to the pile of parts or move them from one department to another. Ford's River Rouge plant looked more like a cluttered and disorganized warehouse than a factory.

The company's management philosophy rankled too. The assembly lines, which were the centrepiece of Ford's pioneering system of mass production, were closely monitored and demanded a labour force of unskilled workers to act like cogs in the machine. The work was boring, repetitive and monotonous. And the workers knew where they stood – at the bottom of the pile. Managers would regularly remind them that they were only needed because they hadn't yet found a machine to replace them with.[2]

Eiji returned to Japan with his ambition intact, but with his admiration for Fordism shattered.

So, following his uncle's tradition, and with the help of his resourceful plant manager Taiichi Ohno, he decided to invent something new. Over the decades that followed, Eiji and colleagues built the Toyota Production System (TPS), the precursor of the modern Lean movement, and one of the most effective business management systems the world has ever seen.[3]

It differed from Fordism in two crucial ways. It focused on eliminating waste, with a one-piece flow production system that was both more flexible and efficient than Ford's batch production method (by necessity, as Toyota didn't have deep pockets from which to fund piles of inventory). And it relied on workers engaging their brains, without someone standing over their shoulder telling them to do so. Each employee was engaged not only with doing their day job, but also with finding ways of doing their day job better – something Eiji called *kaizen*, or continuous improvement.

And it worked. By the time Eiji died in 2013 at the age of 100, Toyota's market capitalization was greater than that of Ford, General Motors and Honda combined.[4] But don't underestimate how difficult it was to make this happen.

You can't just command people to do something and expect it to become a habit. Culture doesn't work that way. People naturally resist change when they have the pressure of day-to-day responsibilities, deadlines and targets.

Fortunately for Toyota – and for us – Eiji was able to figure out a different way of making new ways of working stick, taking inspiration from something you'd expect to find in a place of worship rather than a car factory.

Rituals: Making questions automatic

Everyone who works at Toyota, and the many organizations that have sought to mimic its success, will be familiar with certain set-piece activities that make continuous improvement part of their day-to-day routine.

I (Jen) have never worked on the floor of a Japanese car factory. But in the early days of my consulting career I spent the best part of a year in a giant commercial kitchen, wearing a hairnet and applying the Toyota toolkit to the preparation of ready meals.

Like a car factory, the finished product involved putting all sorts of materials together as you worked your way down the line. But unlike screws and tyres, our materials could go off in a matter of days. Minimising inventory and cutting waste was the name of the game.

Like Toyota, we did *kaizen blitzes*, where we set time aside to brainstorm new ways to cut waste. There were *hansei-kai*, or project post-mortem meetings, and *nemawashi*, where everyone was consulted before big decisions. Then there were *gemba walks* where team members walked the floor so they knew what was happening with their colleagues, and *genchi genbutsu* where senior managers visited the site of a problem so they could see it for themselves.

And it worked. I remember one young kitchen hand who pointed out that if we ordered frozen salmon in packs of 10 instead of 100, we wouldn't be throwing out 50 or 60 salmon on the days where we only needed to defrost a few dozen. And another found a simple solution to our cheese crisis. We'd been adding new crates of cheese to the front of the shelving units and then drawing these fresh stocks down, leaving the cheese behind to grow old and green. He shifted the shelving units away from the wall so we could refill them from the back and draw down from the front. Problem solved.

Ideas like these, which taken together turned the factory around, came from highly choreographed activities lifted straight from the Toyota playbook. And each activity, from the *kaizen blitz* to the *gemba walk*, is best understood as a ritual.

Rituals are often associated with religious and cultural practices – and for good reason. They are sequences of actions that are formulaic, repeatable and imbued with meaning. This makes them powerful. And, as Toyota realized, by designating a time and a place to perform them, they can become a way of life.

As Harvard Business School behavioural scientists Francesca Gino and Michael I. Norton explained in *Scientific American*, "Even simple rituals can be extremely effective. Rituals performed after experiencing losses – from loved ones to lotteries – do alleviate grief, and rituals performed before high-pressure tasks – like singing in public – do in fact reduce anxiety and increase people's confidence. What's more, rituals appear to benefit even people who claim not to believe that rituals work."[5]

If we want to introduce a questioning culture, where the discipline of asking simple but tough questions sticks, then we need to apply the same principle. We must make questioning both hard to avoid and easy to do to a high standard, by ritualizing it.

This needn't involve cramming everyone's calendar with new set-piece activities that promote questioning. Instead, you can reconsecrate what's already in there. It's weekly one-to-ones, quarterly business reviews, board meetings, annual strategy and budgeting cycles, and so on.

If you build each of them around a set of focused, powerful questions – the right QDI play for the job – they can become a platform for the purposeful practice of deep thinking. And those questions – which can cover anything, from generating leap-frog ideas to managing risk to formulating strategy – will then become part of the lexicon of your business, a defining feature of your culture, where everyone knows the words.

Rubber ducks:
The ultimate
questioning rituals

While any of the set piece activities we've mentioned can be useful places to do great thinking, the greatest opportunity lies in the work we do to prepare for them – the reports and presentations we write, and the crib notes we make for ourselves ahead of meetings.

Richard Feynman, the Nobel Prize-winning physicist, showed us why. He took pride in being able to explain profound ideas in simple ways. In the book *Feynman's Lost Lecture*, his former colleague David L. Goodstein retells the story of how one of his most famous lectures came into being.[6]

"Once, I said to him, 'Dick, explain to me, so that I can understand it, why spin one-half particles obey Fermi-Dirac statistics.' Sizing up his audience perfectly, Feynman said, 'I'll prepare a freshman lecture on it.' But he came back a few days later to say, 'I couldn't do it. I couldn't reduce it to the freshman level. That means we don't really understand it.'"

It's only when we attempt to share or externalize our thinking that we are able to scrutinize, sharpen, develop and complete it. Or we realize that we can't.

You don't strictly need other people to help you do this. As visitors to our office will have noticed, we've found rubber ducks do a great job, and rubber-ducking is common practice in tech companies like ours. When debugging code, you find an inanimate object like a rubber duck, plonk it on the desk next to you and explain to it what the problem is. The duck stays schtum, but it's the same principle – by getting your ideas out of your head, you can hold your thinking up to inspection and ask yourself the hard questions that are necessary for you to properly understand them.

Most of the time, thinking out loud means writing things down rather than talking to a duck. Which makes preparing a report or presentation for a set-piece activity like a management or board meeting a golden opportunity to get your thinking straight. As you refine your output, you refine your thinking. With every draft, it gets stronger.

It doesn't take much to get going. All that's required is to tailor a QDI play or question set to the ritual, and turn it into the backbone of your preparation and the conversation. In a performance review, for example, it's as simple as asking yourself, "What went well and why?", "What are you most worried about?" and "What are we going to stop, start or do differently as a result?"

Everyone has the raw materials: diaries full of set-piece activities and teams stacked with grey matter. But these activities only turn into Toyota-style rituals when you supercharge them with QDI plays. Without QDI plays, they're a drag on everyone's time. With them,

they become the place where deep thinking happens –
and you're on a path to collective intelligence.

———————

You've embraced the power of questions and rituals and
used the odd rubber duck. You've built an organization
in which everyone is in the habit of asking more and
better questions. Insights and ideas are emerging at
every level.

There's only one problem. What if nobody's listening?

Part II

Communication

How will Part II help you build collective intelligence?

Effective communication – the sort that gets good thinking out of people's heads so others can act on it – is difficult and we're terrible at it. Without it, great thinking withers on the vine. To get better at it, we have to throw out some long-held beliefs about what makes good communication and acquire new habits. In Part II, we'll show you what they are and how to do it.

———— BOTTOM LINE UP FRONT ————

Chapter 4

(Mis) communication

What happens when good thinking meets poor communication?

"That doesn't seem right, does it?"

Captain Larry Wheaton and co-pilot Roger Pettit watched in silence as the de-icing truck pulled up beside their Boeing 737. The snow was still falling, as the high-pressure stream of mixed ethylene glycol and water lashed their wings and fuselage, creating a fine mist that only added to the whiteout.[1]

Wheaton gave the passengers an update. They were restless and who could blame them? No one likes waiting, especially when they had tickets to take them away from the blizzards of Washington DC to the winter sun of Fort Lauderdale.

An hour and a half behind schedule, on January 13 1982, Air Florida flight 90 finally received clearance to taxi from the control tower for what would turn out to be the last flight that Wheaton and Pettit would ever take.

At first the plane wouldn't budge. The snow, ice and spilt de-icing fluid made it too slippery. Wheaton and Pettit – both in their early 30s, with plenty of flight hours logged – put the engines into reverse thrust to get things moving, which did little more than blow snow and slush around and back onto the plane.

Eventually a tug with chains on its tyres was driven under the 737 and a tow bar attached to the wheel.

"We'll see you later," yelled the tug operator into his mic, as the plane began to ease back from the terminal. "Righto," replied Wheaton.

Having taxied toward the runway, the pilots were then forced to wait while the other aircraft queued ahead of them took off.

An hour passed since the de-icing, while snow continued to land gently on the wings. In the cockpit, the recording device picked up the conversation between Pettit and Wheaton. "Boy this is shitty," said Pettit. "It's probably the shittiest snow I've seen."

Finally, at 15:57, they were cleared for take-off. Pettit cranked up the engines which screamed into life, and they set off along the frozen runway. From this point, the pilots now had 47 precious seconds to make a final decision on whether to press ahead or abort.

"Look at how the ice is just hanging ... back there, see that? See all those icicles on the back there and everything?" Pettit said, over the plane's rattle.

"Yeah," Wheaton said.

"Boy ... this is a losing battle here on trying to de-ice those things ... [it gives] a false feeling of security, that's all it does," Pettit continued, but this time Wheaton didn't reply.

It was taking longer than usual to build the necessary thrust and the plane raced further and further down the runway, way past the point where most aircraft would have taken off. The flight recorder picked up the fragmented conversation that happened next.

Pettit:	"That doesn't seem right, does it?"
Wheaton:	"Yes it is, there's 80."
Pettit:	"No I don't think that's right ... maybe it is."
Wheaton:	"Hundred and twenty."
Pettit:	"I don't know ..."

The plane was airborne for 30 seconds before it stalled and crashed into the icy Potomac River, killing 70 of the 74 passengers on board and four crew members, including both pilots. According to one eyewitness it shattered "like an egg cracked on the side of a dish." Other eyewitnesses spoke of an eerie silence right after impact, as the waters slowly pulled what was left of Air Florida 90 out of sight.

———————

I (Jen) first read about the Air Florida 90 disaster thirty years later, while I was waiting to board a flight to the snowiest part of Sweden.

As I flicked through a magazine, my eyes rested on the pilots' college yearbook photos and the grainy images taken at the scene of the crash. I hoped it wasn't an omen. And, selfishly, as I walked up the steps to board my flight, I hoped that lessons had been learned, making it less likely to happen again.

Various factors were said to have contributed to the disaster, such as the weather and the decision to reverse thrusters in the snow. But the subsequent investigation also revealed another contributing factor: that the pilots had failed to communicate with clarity and impact.[2]

Pettit did try to convey his doubts, four times sharing observations and anomalous engine readings that were each sufficient reason enough to abort. But his indirect and hesitant communication style failed to cut through.

Lecturer Chad Plenge runs programmes for high potential leaders in the US Army's Center for Junior Officers. As he says, "If the first officer of flight 90 had simply stated, 'There is ice building up on the wings, so we need to deice again," the disaster would likely have been averted."[3]

How you say something matters just as much as what you say.

Communicating well – saying things the right way – is an essential skill in all circumstances. Business is no exception. Without it, the fruits of curiosity and critical thinking die on the vine. Powerful insights and compelling ideas can be ignored if the messages conveying them are vague, ambiguous or unclear.

It's not just threats that we can miss. Xerox famously developed the first PC in 1973 – the Alto, complete with mouse, graphical display, icons, ethernet networking and scalable type – but failed to commercialize on the opportunity, allowing Apple and IBM to swoop in and launch the digital age.[4]

According to the book *Fumbling the Future: How Xerox Invented, Then Ignored, the First Personal Computer*, by Robert Alexander and Douglas Smith, the failure was largely due to the isolation of the Alto team from senior management and other departments.[5] Because they weren't talking with each other, it meant they were unable to see the commercial potential that leaders of other business divisions could have told them about, unable to get buy-in from those who controlled the budget, and either unwilling or unaware of the need to get patent protection for some of their ground-breaking innovations.

Great ideas don't always float to the surface – and there's no guarantee they'll be acted on and developed if they do. To think better, we need to know what others know and benefit from their observations and perspectives. To turn that thinking into timely action, we need it to reach and convince those who have the capacity to act on it. For collective intelligence to work you, therefore, need your people to express themselves with consistent clarity and impact.

Communication breakdown, it's always the same

Unfortunately, communicating well is difficult – and most of us are not very good at it. Examples of this are found everywhere.

Better.com CEO Vishal Garg went viral for all the wrong reasons in 2021 when he laid off 900 employees in an awkward, monotone, one-way Zoom call.[6] Like a robot reading a grocery list from a piece of paper on his desk, he told his shocked employees that they no longer had jobs. "This is the second time in my career I'm doing this, and I do not want to do this. The last time I did it, I cried; this time I hope to be stronger," he confessed.

It triggered social media outrage and several senior executives resigned. "I own the decision to do the lay-offs, but in communicating it, I blundered the execution," he later said in an apology issued on the company's blog (not by video, unsurprisingly).

If you think writing things down makes it easier, think again. We've spent the last 15 years immersed in the most important written documents that businesses produce – their board papers. These underpin the highest-level thinking in a business, providing the raw material for discussions about an organization's biggest issues by arguably its brightest and most experienced minds.

Typically they're anywhere from 200 to 1,000 slides or pages of the most impenetrable, labyrinthine stuff you'll ever read.

When we had our first meeting with Sir Sandie Crombie, a veteran director whose firm had just brought us in to revamp their board deck, he pointed to his face and said "This is not the face of a very old man. This is just the face of a man who has ploughed through 5,500 pages in the last two days." Having spoken to hundreds of others in his shoes and waded through the documents he was referring to, we could feel his pain.

It isn't just a volume problem. Board decks usually comprise dozens of inconsistently presented reports, the worst swollen with charts, presentations, tables, rambling text slabs and footnotes in ant trail font.* One recently had something resembling a Gantt chart with about 80 rows and 25 columns, running horizontally across five pages. We still haven't figured out what it was about because they forgot the key.

Board decks are so full of noise that, for leaders, finding the vital signals in them is next to impossible, like picking up a whisper next to a busy street.

The problem doesn't just exist in the boardroom. Poor board materials are often indicative of a pervasive communication problem within the organization at large, with layer upon layer of reporting creating thick fog from the executive committee downwards. A bank executive told us that he'd once stacked his weekend's reading on the dining table at home, just for fun, and the pile of papers measured at over a foot high.

These problems tend to get worse as businesses grow. The larger and more complex a business, the harder it is for important messages to cut through its layers and be understood. No wonder that poor communication is described in some quarters as the "silent killer of big companies."[7] Indeed, our work with Fortune 500 firms confirms that it plagues even those businesses that supposedly have access to the best and most focused information money can buy.

So how do you solve a problem like that?

°   Ant trail font - otherwise known as size 4 Arial - looks like this

Good communicators are ~~born~~ made

You can learn a lot about a person from their social media feeds. It's clear that the algorithms have decided that one of us (Pippa) is in need of some serious communication help, regularly serving up snippets of encouragement.

> **"The single biggest problem in communication is the illusion that it has taken place."**
> ~ George Bernard Shaw

> **"Blessed is the man who, having nothing to say, abstains from giving wordy evidence of the fact."**
> ~ George Eliot

> **"I am so clever that sometimes I don't understand a single word of what I am saying."**
> ~ Oscar Wilde

All very inspiring, but not particularly helpful. In general, the quest for advice to improve communication skills seems to regularly stall at some witty, pithy variant of 'do it better' from someone (like Shaw, Eliot, or Wilde) who finds it easy to do it better. I'm left feeling more motivated but none the wiser as to what to do about it.

The reason my social media feeds are full of this is because for my whole life I have felt the pressing need to get better at communication.

When it comes to this, as with much else, the two of us are chalk and cheese. Jen genuinely enjoys writing. I *hate* it. It has never come naturally to me. When I was seven, my parents were summoned to the local primary school and told, "I'm afraid she's just not that bright. She's failing her English."

A dyslexia diagnosis and years of special support followed, but I never grew to be a wordsmith. I stuck to numbers, training as a scientist before moving into finance, and I still wince whenever anyone asks me what's on my bookshelves (spoiler: it's not books). Yet this didn't stop me from learning how to write well when I needed to.

I had a shock when Jen and I founded our business and I needed to read our clients' board papers. I could make neither head nor tail of them. My imposter syndrome raged until I realized that I wasn't alone – nobody else could either, including the board members and executives they were written for. The CFO of a FTSE 100 company once confided that even he didn't understand his company's finance report.

All of these organizations employed plenty of natural wordsmiths, as well as numbersmiths like me, to produce this information. And yet what they were producing was drivel.

Like any well-trained scientist I wanted to understand why – to break the problem down so I could fix it. I discovered that convention was getting in our way. The tenets of good communication that we all learned at school and that were reinforced at work were, quite simply, the wrong ones.

So, the solution seemed obvious: replace those dud conventions with new ones. Write some new rules that actually work. With Jen, I have spent over a decade testing and iterating them, experimenting with thousands of executives across hundreds of organizations. Now, finally, having turned work into my laboratory, this numbers person has found the formula for how to write.

If I can do it, anyone can. You needn't be born a great communicator; it's a skill you can develop, just like critical thinking. By cultivating this skill throughout their organization and 'making' great communicators, leaders can help people to share their thinking and give it to others to act on.

So, what conventions have we relegated to history's dustbin? And just as importantly, what have we replaced them with?

Chapter 5

Conventions

What do we need to unlearn?

For years, we've been battling against the following five conventions, each deeply entrenched in how we communicate in business and each deeply unhelpful. In this chapter we'll share what they are, why you need to unlearn them, and the new rules we want to put in their place.

Let's jump straight in.

Convention 1

~~A slick presentation is a decision-maker's best friend.~~

The pen is mightier than the slide deck.

Having spent 15 years wading through our clients' slide decks – pretty ones that tell you nothing and over-crowded ones that leave you feeling dizzy – we've seen first-hand how often they're misused, giving muddled thinking a cloak of respectability.

We're not the only ones. At Amazon at some point in 2004, someone lost to history delivered a PowerPoint presentation that finally drove Jeff Bezos over the edge. Fed up with slide decks, he penned a short note to his senior team explaining that they were officially and permanently banned. Instead, when discussing reports or proposals, the person or team responsible would write a two-to-six-page memo.

"The narrative structure of a good memo forces better thought and better understanding of what's more important than what, and how things are related," his note read.[1] "PowerPoint-style presentations somehow give permission to gloss over ideas, flatten out any sense of relative importance, and ignore the interconnectedness of ideas."

Even the humble bullet point got the chop: the Amazon founder wanted his business to be run on whole paragraphs. "Narratively structured memos are harder to write because they require better thinking. It's worth it."[2]

Bezos' beef with bullet points was well-founded. Research from the University of Central Lancashire discovered that they overload the brain, by forcing us to consume too much information at once and making it difficult for us to logically separate and then remember distinct concepts.[3]

They can look and sound convincing, particularly when delivered with aplomb, but that just makes it harder for others to scrutinize the reasoning behind them. Indeed, by banning presentations, Bezos had clocked something we've seen play out time and again in boardrooms – charisma and slick delivery masking poor quality thinking and execution, and great ideas floundering when presented by wallflowers.

Don't get us wrong. There's a time and a place for a rousing speech or presentation – townhalls, annual kick-offs, conferences, investor and customer pitches, and so on. When you're sending troops into battle you can't rely on a pithy memo to fire them up. But we're not talking about how to fire up a group around a decision that has been taken. We're talking about how you transmit high-quality critical thinking to peers and the powers that be, so that they can engage with it, challenge and refine it, and, ideally, decide to act on it.

By demanding written memos with fully-fledged thinking, Bezos launched Amazon on its journey to a narrative-driven business.[4] Bezos later described the decision to adopt a writing culture as "probably the smartest thing we ever did."[5]

He's not the only leader to have had this epiphany. When US Army Brigadier General H. R. McMaster's forces secured the northern Iraqi city of Tal Afar in 2005, he banned PowerPoint presentations, calling the software an "internal threat."

"It's dangerous because it can create the illusion of understanding and the illusion of control," he later explained.[6] General James N. Mattis of the US Marine Corps put it more simply: "PowerPoint makes us stupid."

Writing cultures aren't just the preserve of the military and Amazon. You can also find them in places like Stripe,[7] Slack, Square, Dropbox, Airbnb, TripAdvisor, Basecamp and SAP, as well as in our business and the wide variety of businesses we work with.[8] Each has recognized that narrative prose provides the ideal medium not only to encourage good thinking but also to convert it into action.

Writing cultures really take off when individuals realize how effective narrative communication can be, as Rob Enslin tells us. When Rob and I (Jen) first met, he'd been introduced to me as "the hypergrowth guy." And for good reason. As President of Google Cloud, he took on the incumbents AWS and Microsoft Azure and doubled its revenue in two years. Before that, he was part of the executive team that grew SAP from $450m to $30bn revenue, and it was there that he picked up the writing bug – out of necessity.

In his early 30s, while running SAP's Coca-Cola account, Enslin saw the need for a major course correction but struggled to get his point across. "I could see I wasn't getting through to people by just talking my plan through. I needed my boss and my team to listen to my full logic and get bought into my thinking. I could do that with a written report," Enslin says.

"For six weeks I spent every night at my computer typing away. I'd be up until after 11pm, writing, writing, writing," he says. Eventually he boiled it down to a short document. "I delivered it to my boss and said, 'We have to change things. This project is going to fail. Here I've written it down for you. I need you to read it.'"

Ever since then, Enslin has spent hours writing to get his thoughts straightened out, both to understand what he thinks and so that others can see exactly what he means. "I'll sit at my computer, writing, reading, re-reading and re-rewriting, until the idea or plan crystallizes into a 1-2 pager," he says. "Now, I ask the people that work for me to do the same."

Convention 2

~~Good stories have a beginning, middle and end,
and the end is where you land your punch.~~

Hit them with key messages first.

Let us tell you the story of how almost every book you've ever read goes.

In *the beginning*, the writer sets a scene, pulling back the veil on the main characters and introducing the fateful conflict that will change their world forever. The writer then leads you into *the middle*, where the plot thickens and twists, and the now-familiar protagonists battle their demons. Drama and intrigue keep you on the edge of your seat, flipping pages until the writer guides you to *the end*, a satisfying place where the conflict is resolved, loose ends are tied up in a neat bow and everyone lives happily ever after.

Almost every story follows this pattern, from Gilgamesh through to Romeo and Juliet, Spiderman, and Borat. Jokes do much the same thing – set-up (*'Knock knock'* ... *'Who's there?'*), development (*'Who.'* ... *'Who who?'*), punchline (*'What are you, an owl?'*).

We're taught to follow the same three-layered 'hamburger' recipe when writing stories in primary school, all the way through to academic essays at university: introduction, analysis, conclusion.

It should be no surprise that this approach seeps into business writing too. Reports typically start by providing some background, then go into the detail before sharing the insight or recommendation at the end. Presentation decks similarly build to a big reveal, summarizing the key takeaways on the final slide.

We've spent thousands of hours chomping through communications structured this way, coming out the other side with only one clear thought – we're sick of hamburgers.

Business writing should be more like a *smørrebrød*, the Danish open sandwich. Put your conclusion up front (the pickled herring and cucumber topping). Then show what your conclusion is based on and how you got there – the strength and rigour underpinning the thinking (the rye bread).

Here's why.

Key messages need to be shouted from the rooftop, not hidden in the haystack.

Holding back the vital information for the conclusion and putting the Bottom Line At the Bottom (the BLAB), only makes sense if the reader is going to stay with you long enough to get that far. Even if executives do reach the end of a report, there's no guarantee they'll come away with the key points that the writer intended. It's perilously easy to get lost or distracted along the way. They need help to find the signal in the noise.

In the military, where getting your point across can be a matter of life and death, they call it putting the Bottom Line Up Front (the BLUF). There's little value in giving your commander a detailed report of the situation on the front line and waiting until page 40 to reveal that you're under attack. You have to get the big idea across first.

This doesn't mean that business communication will be dull or dry – quite the opposite. In fact, the great stories we listed earlier don't follow a strict 'hamburger' structure at all. We all know that Spiderman will make it out alive, and Romeo and Juliet will not. It doesn't make the story less enjoyable; it heightens the suspense. As Hitchcock said, "There is no terror in the bang, only in the anticipation of it." It's only if you know what's going to happen that you'll be on the edge of your seat wondering how the author or director will get you there.

Journalists, who know a thing or two about good writing and how to draw you in, have long operated on the same principle, using a 'nut graph' to grab readers' attention early on.

Oliver Shah, associate editor at *The Sunday Times*, best-selling author, and former Business Journalist of the Year, described this to us as "a nuts-and-bolts paragraph, where in three sentences you tell the reader exactly what the piece is about." In the cut-and-thrust of the news business, "It's essential to help your reader work out if they want to read on, and save them time if they don't," Shah explains.

Putting the Bottom Line Up Front is one thing, but working out what the BLUF should say – and reinforcing it with detail that shows the thinking behind it is sound – is easier said than done. We've read plenty of attempts at pithy summaries that misfire – where the key points don't do themselves justice, and the rest of the report is a messy quagmire. So how do you do it?

All good communication, as with good thinking, should know what questions it's answering. And those questions are the load-bearing structure on which you hang everything you want to say. If you've developed QDI plays, they're the place to start.

Begin with the 'in a nutshell' answers to each of those questions. Spell out each question and answer each one in turn. Treat those answers like an elevator pitch to a bored 15-year-old. If you only had 30 seconds to explain what you think and why they should care, before they put their earphones back in, what would you say?

One vital addition before you dive into more detail is to make an ask of your audience, directly requesting something from them. Sharing information should always be a two-way exchange of value, so it's important to prime the audience to give you something back (insights, resources, ideas) before they slump into passive receiver mode.

Then, after the BLUF and the audience question, comes the detail – unpacking each of those questions layer by layer, until you're sure your audience has followed your thinking and understands why you drew the conclusions you did. By using those questions as subheadings in the report, the detail after the BLUF becomes easier to follow and more compelling. Studies show that blog titles phrased as questions are more likely to be clicked on than those without.[9] They pique readers' curiosity, which is exactly what you need to do if you want them to get to the end.

> ## Convention 3
>
> ~~Serious subjects demand formal writing.~~
>
> Write like a human being,
> no matter what you're writing about.

A scene in a 2003 episode of *Friends* opens with Joey sitting in front of a laptop, racking his brains over a letter of recommendation he's writing to the "baby adoption decider people."[10]

He wants them to know how great his friends Monica and Chandler are. He wants to say that they'd make perfect parents. But he doesn't know how. "I want it to sound smart, but I don't know any big words," he admits to another friend, Ross.

Ross offers a simple solution: "Why don't you use a thesaurus?" Joey's never heard of one, but when Ross shows him what it can do, he's impressed. He cracks on with the letter and a couple of hours later strides confidently into Monica and Chandler's apartment, declaring, "I think you'll be very, very happy."

Monica and Chandler begin to read the letter.

Chandler: *(reading, frowning)*
I don't ... uh ... understand.

Joey: Some of the words are a little too sophisticated for ya?

Monica: *(also reading it, also frowning)*
It doesn't make any sense.

Joey: Of course it does! It's smart!
I used the the-saurus!

Chandler: On every word?

Joey: Yep!

Monica: Alright, what was this sentence originally? (shows the sentence to Joey)

Joey: Oh, 'They are warm, nice, people with big hearts.'

Chandler: And that became 'they are humid prepossessing Homo Sapiens with full sized aortic pumps'?

Joey: Yeah, and hey, I really mean it, dude.

Monica: Joey, I don't think we can use this.

Joey: Why not?

Monica: Well, because you signed it baby kangaroo Tribbiani.

The scene ends with Chandler pleading with Joey to re-write the letter from his "full-sized aortic pump," to peals of laughter from the studio audience.

Like with all great comedy, this scene from *Friends* tickles the funny bone because it's based in truth. We're not just laughing at Joey; we're laughing at ourselves and everyone else we've seen make the same mistake.

When we sit down to write something important, something comes over us. We stop communicating normally and start communicating the way we think we're supposed to. Our tone becomes formal. We try to sound clever and authoritative in the words we choose and the way we use them.

It's only natural. Lawyers, academics and authority figures do it all the time. We all know that if you want other people to take you and your topic seriously, you need to sound smart, right?

Well, as Joey's experience shows, sophisticated words can make you sound stupid.

As much as we might enjoy revisiting 90s sitcoms, the implications are far from a laughing matter. In Monica and Chandler's case, they might have missed out on becoming parents. In business, this convention is so religiously applied that vast swathes of information – which could contain vital insights – are at best being skimmed and are rarely understood fully.

If, instead of picking up a thesaurus, Joey had read this chapter, he'd have found that to sound smart he needed to sound human and choose words that would help his thinking shine. And he'd have found three essential tips to help him do it.

Tip 1: Use short, simple words and sentences

Over 70 years ago, writer Rudolf Flesch figured out that long sentences and multi-syllable words place extra strain on our working memory – extra cognitive load.[11] To this day, his discovery is at the heart of almost all modern readability calculators.[12]

Not only do shorter words and sentences make life easier for your audience, they also make you look good. Countless studies across countries and cultures, from Princeton to the University of Tokyo, show this.[13, 14] Time and again, researchers have found that if you ask someone to score the intelligence of an author based on a passage of text, the authors who use shorter words and sentences are the ones who come out on top. We're sure Princeton's Daniel Oppenheimer had his tongue firmly in cheek, and perhaps Joey's thesaurus at hand, when he titled his research paper 'Consequences of Erudite Vernacular Utilized Irrespective of Necessity.'

Instead of:	Try this instead:
concerning	about
utilize	use
is able to	can
frequently	often

Tip 2: Use the first person, active voice

Dame Mary Beard, the celebrated classical historian, admits that she too suffered from the mistaken belief that "formality ... was the stamp of authority" in the early part of her career – and it meant she struggled to produce anything that cut through.[15]

One day, she got a wake-up call. "A friend read something I had written and was brave enough to say, 'this is probably right, but it's boring.' It wasn't nice to hear, but it was true," she recalls. She went on to write her 600-page history of Rome, *SPQR*, "in my own voice ... trying to interest the imaginary audience in front of me." It worked – the book became a best-seller and propelled Beard onto prime-time television and the board of the British Museum.

The secret sauce – for Beard, as well as other famously good communicators like Warren Buffett, Jack Welch and Barack Obama – was that she found her voice. Their personalities and perspectives seep into their words. People feel that they are speaking to them.

A simple way to do this is to use the first person, active voice – "I'll process your order," rather than, "Your order will be processed."

One way to avoid slipping into the passive voice is to use neobank Monzo's nifty 'by monkeys' mantra.[16] If you add '... by monkeys' to the end of a statement and it still makes sense, you're being passive. (Compare "A decision was made to close your account ...

by monkeys" with "I have decided to close your account ... by monkeys.")

This not only makes for a more engaging read, it also encourages management to own their message – a display of accountability that is crucial for getting others to lean in and back their ideas. If colleagues sense you're hiding out of view (for example, by saying, "Sales targets were missed," rather than, "We missed our sales targets"), they're much less likely to buy into what you're telling them, or to give you the support or resources you need.

Instead of:	Try this instead:
An appointment will be scheduled	I'll make an appointment
Key project milestones were missed	We missed key project milestones
A thorough investigation will be conducted	Our HR team will conduct a thorough investigation

Tip 3: Bin the jargon

Jargon can save time, but it can also cause problems by making your thinking inaccessible.

Journalists take a particularly hard line on this. "It's obviously a no-no for us but, in business, jargon can be used to obfuscate – to make it hard to see what is really going on," explains the *Financial Times*' senior business writer, Andrew Hill. Although it has a place in certain highly specialized environments, for example, within surgical teams, "it becomes dangerous when it gets out in the wild and then sticks."

So, beware of using it. And, if you absolutely must, be sure to define it clearly wherever it first appears.

Convention 4

~~Data speaks for itself, driving powerful insights.~~

Questions drive insights.
Use data to help answer them.

Late one evening, at a local tavern, a drunk man finally decides to call it a night. He steps outside and takes a deep breath. It's murky and still, with thick black clouds and no moon. Home is ten minutes away, down a dank alley.

He stumbles along it, barely able to see where he's going, stopping occasionally to catch his balance against a damp brick wall. Eventually he sees the lamplight outside his building and makes his way over.

When he gets there, he starts fumbling around in his coat pocket for his keys. After about half a minute, he lets out a groan, that becomes a roar, that becomes an outburst of his finest swear words. He must have dropped them. Sighing, he bends down and starts to look.

A passer-by offers to help, and the two search fruitlessly for the next half-hour, scouring the area around the lamp post for any sign of the keys. Reaching the end of his patience, the passer-by eventually asks, "Are you sure you lost your keys here?"

"Oh no," says the drunk man, shaking his head and pointing to the darker part of the alley. "I probably lost them over there. But there's no way we're going to find them there, it's too dark."

When it comes to using data to shape our thinking and drive insight, we're no different from the hapless man. He went looking for the answer to his problem, his lost keys, in the glare of the streetlight a few yards from his front door. It was inconvenient to retrace his steps at such a late hour, and he had no appetite for fumbling in the dark where he'd stumbled – and where his keys were likely to be found.

In business, we too default to crunching and presenting the data that's readily accessible, rather than chasing down the data we really need that's harder to get hold of. And, these days, there's no shortage of data within easy reach.

In 2006, mathematician and entrepreneur Clive Humby declared, "data is the new oil."[17] Now there are whole industries dedicated to helping us gather, clean, integrate, analyse, mine, model, visualize and report it. And the coolest companies pride themselves on their so-called data-driven decision-making.

But rather than helping us find and then illuminate the insights that matter, it's blinding us – and giving us the false sense of security that, by using data lots, we're using the right data or using it well.

Questions drive insights, not data. So, you should only use data if it helps to answer a question that matters. If you're not clear what question your data is answering, then you probably shouldn't include it. And when you do include it, make clear what you and your audience can learn from it and remember that less is often more.

We saw the value of this when we worked with a FTSE 100 consumer services business. While everyone else was trying to talk about the big picture, one senior director seemed fixated on dissecting profitability data for their 1,000 service lines. He wanted to see every imaginable metric and cut of performance data, for every single one.

What a board director wants, a board director gets. So, to the bafflement of the rest of the board, the despairing finance team responded by sharing reams of statistics, charts and graphics for each board meeting, bloating the board pack to unreadable proportions.

We'd never seen such attention to detail, and – admirable though this quality can be at other times – it seemed thoroughly counterproductive here. We were curious: what question was he trying to answer?

After a frank conversation, he asked us to leave him alone for 15 minutes while he had a stab at making sense of it for us. We went and got a coffee, and by the time we came back to the room he had three questions scrawled on a sheet of paper in front of him. Those questions were:

1. Are we increasing the capacity of our most profitable service lines?
2. Are we reducing our exposure to our least profitable ones?
3. Where we are not, is there a good reason? For example, to pump prime a new service line while it finds its feet.

All very sensible questions. But, by not being explicit about the questions on his mind, he overwhelmed his colleagues with detail that made it hard to find answers to the questions that mattered and often led the board discussion down a rabbit hole.

Fortunately, the fix was a simple one. A single chart on half a side of A4 replaced 35 pages of spreadsheets, which totally missed the point. This one chart plotted the service lines by profitability and whether they were in the process of having capacity added or removed.

But of course, this only tackled the first two of the director's questions. The third was answered by management in narrative, on the bottom half of said sheet of A4. And it forced management to grapple with a difficult question that everyone, including the CEO, agreed was worth their effort.

Less is more

Most internal business communications – reports, papers, presentations, emails – are just too long. Saying less is hard, but it's worth the time and the effort.

First of all, a shorter paper is more likely to be read because we aren't disheartened by the length of it. Secondly, it makes the author look good. Long, rambling communications raise suspicion. Is the author trying to bury critical information? Or do they lack the smarts to sort wheat from chaff?

To cut your report or email down to size, don't chop away with abandon. Instead, start by working out what question or questions you're trying to answer in whatever you're writing. This will stop you from straying into 'information for information's' sake, the cause of many a bloated report. A QDI play will often provide a good starting point.

Then go wide before you go deep. Back in Part 1 we suggested you map out your thinking visually, as a family tree, to help make sure you don't miss a question and to organize all the sub-questions each one throws off. When you come to write up this visual map, think of it like organizing a wedding guest list. You might not have space for everyone on the family tree, but if you want to avoid drama you need to include everyone at whatever level you go down to. You wouldn't invite one cousin and not the others.

Similarly, in a report or email you must first cover all the primary building blocks at the top level of your tree, answering each of the highest-level questions. Together these represent the full breadth of your argument or analysis. After that you can unpack each of those building blocks, working through the layers of thinking or evidence that underpin each one. You can choose how many layers deep you go, but you always go the full width of the tree. The trade-off is one of detail not coverage.

For disruptive energy provider Octopus Energy, doing all of this has been key to taming the reporting beast and raising the bar. They used to follow a rigid format full of prescribed metrics for their weekly management pack, but questioned its value when it ballooned in size. Now, they ask the team to start with a question instead: 'what matters?'

As founding team member Pete Miller told us, "They'll now say to each other, 'I don't quite get this, we should look into it further,' or 'There's something missing here, we need to go deeper.'" The team are using their brains and their judgement to work out what matters and what doesn't – a sought-after leadership trait.

Convention 5

~~Meetings are a drain – purge them.~~

Meetings are vital – use them wisely.

"Meetings are where minutes are taken and hours are wasted," goes the popular saying, sometimes attributed to the fictional 23rd-century spaceship commander Captain James T. Kirk.

Many would agree with him. A University of North Carolina study found that a third of meetings across over 20 industries were completely unnecessary, costing large companies over $100m a year.[17] Another, from Harvard Business School, found that only 17% of senior executives considered meetings a productive use of group or individual time – which is problematic given they spend on average 23 hours a week in them.[18]

No wonder so many organizations – including Shopify, Meta, Tesla, Clorox, Atom Bank, Bolt and Twilio – have taken a scythe to their calendars. They've scrapped recurring meetings with more than two or three people, instituted no-meeting days and limited meetings to 30-45 minutes to reduce the burden.

"No one joined Shopify to sit in meetings," declared the firm's COO Kaz Nejatian in an all-staff email announcing its 'calendar purge' in early 2023.[19]

Productivity hacks like this are catnip to stressed out, overworked executives and their teams. And the leaders behind these purges are hailed for boldly going where no leaders have gone before, giving people their time and headspace back.

We're not so sure.

By scrapping meetings, are these leaders solving the right problem? Their companies may have fewer, shorter meetings but they won't suddenly become *good* meetings. And what new problems are they creating by taking them away?

Don't get us wrong, as working parents we're as keen as anyone to spend less time in meetings. And, as co-CEOs of a software business that helps make asynchronous working work, it would serve our interests to jump on the bandwagon and encourage everyone to follow suit.

But we don't think you should, because this is one of those cures, like surgically extracting infected teeth in the 17th century, that is worse than the disease.

Meetings are vital. Not just for building culture and connections (increasingly important in a hybrid working world), but for stimulating dialogue and, with it, collective intelligence. If you want a happy, motivated and connected workforce, you need to bring people together. If you want that workforce to deliver more than the sum of its parts, you need to bring them together *better*.

Doing meetings better means equipping people to be effective in them. As we've already seen in this book, you can't rely on smart people to think or communicate well as individuals. Why on earth would we expect them to, when you shove them together and leave them to it?

After helping hundreds of organizations and thousands of leaders with their meetings over the past 15 years, we've learned that those with the best meetings stick to three rules.

Rule 1: Build meetings around questions

Everything benefits from structure. The human body without a skeleton would be nothing more than a flabby, floppy pile of organs.

Meetings are no different. Without structure – in this case, an agenda – they're circular marathons of chit-chat, cross-speak, and tangents.

Unfortunately, even though most meetings of any substance do have an agenda, they still feel frustratingly unproductive. So, what are we getting wrong?

We're building, and using, them the wrong way.

We need to see the agenda less as a time management device, and more as the fundamental structure for everything that comes before, during and after the meeting. The key to this is to phrase each agenda item as a question.

Meetings are great rituals for asking and answering questions, and making that explicit reminds everyone that they're there to use their brains. It makes it easier for the organizer to pick the right group of people to answer them. And by expressing each agenda item as a question, you'll frame the preparation, information gathering, discussion and actions.

The sequencing of agenda items is important too. Some questions on the agenda will demand 'divergent thinking' (generating ideas and possibilities – the realm of curiosity), others 'convergent thinking' (evaluating, analysing and forming judgements – analytical territory). Repeatedly switching between one thinking style and the other is exhausting and hard to do well, so to get the best from your attendees, try not to.

Group together the agenda questions (or conversations) based on the type of thinking they demand, so you tackle divergent thinking questions separately from those that require convergent thinking. Where possible, hold the discussions on separate days – or at the very least separated by a meaningful break.

The chair of one of the largest hospitals in the UK went further. He rebadged every second board meeting a 'Thinking Day' to signal the style of conversation that was expected. It created an environment conducive to everyone in the room – management and the board – participating as equals, without repeatedly breaking the collegiate atmosphere to scrutinize and challenge.

Finally, we need to keep the agenda short. With long 'shopping list' agendas you're more likely to fail to cover the ground you need to, or rush through the items superficially. If you want to go deep, it's perfectly acceptable to limit the agenda to one question. In fact, we'd suggest doing so whenever you can.

Rule 2: Build meetings around dialogue

Two and a half millennia ago, our old friend Socrates gave a glimpse of what great meetings look like. His symposia may have had rather more wine and dancing than would be professional today, but they were none-theless genuine meetings of minds – occasions for dialogue and discussion.

Time is precious, but meeting time also presents a unique opportunity – to engage in Socratic-style dialogue and do some of your organization's best thinking. Unfortunately, we often squander that opportunity by spending meeting time on things that could be done in advance. Like listening to presentations, for example.

In 2007, two Colorado-based science teachers, Jon Bergmann and Aaron Sams, shared a similar frustration.

But their problem wasn't with meetings. They were obsessed with how to optimize face-to-face time with their students in the classroom.

As Bergmann says, "For 24 years I was a high school science teacher. I would send the kids home to do their homework. And they would get stuck."[20] Their parents couldn't remember enough high-school chemistry to be of much help. It dawned on Bergmann and Sams that *this* was when the children needed them most – when they applied the theory and reached the limit of their understanding. But, instead of being able to help them push through whatever was blocking them, the teachers were at home, tucking into their dinner and marking the previous day's homework. By using classroom time with their students to, "yak at them and give them content," were the teachers wasting a vital opportunity to help them learn?

"We asked ourselves, 'Are there better ways for kids to learn these things?' We went back and examined everything we did," Bergmann later told *The Washington Post.*[21]

What they discovered was the 'flipped classroom' model. Rather than lecturing students in the classroom and sending them away to apply what they've learned in their homework, this approach 'flips' it around. YouTube was still in its infancy, but Sams was browsing a technology magazine when he read about a way to record and distribute PowerPoint presentations complete with voice and annotations. So, in the spring of 2007 he and Bergmann tried it out, recording their lessons and asking students to watch them and to study supporting texts as 'homework.' The students would then apply the learnings in the classroom, making best use of the teacher's presence to help them when they got stuck and to cement and deepen their understanding through discussion.

It was so effective that Bergmann and Sams have published books[22] extolling the virtues and thousands of schools and educational districts have since adopted it.[23]

The 'flipped' model has a similarly enlivening effect on meetings too, by ensuring time together is used not to fill heads with information but to push the group's thinking forward.

This means sharing information in advance with a concise, compelling pre-read based on the relevant QDI play to get everyone on the same page. Before you even arrive in the room together, clarification questions can be raised and resolved. Whoever will lead the meeting can also gather discussion points, ideas and concerns in advance to help them plan and guide the conversation. Meeting time is then used to best effect – to do the thinking we can only do together.

Rule 3: Set traps for your meeting gremlins

Great conversations surface different views and uncomfortable truths without descending into warfare. But this won't happen by itself, and even the most diverse groups can fall foul of bias, groupthink and an unhealthy fear of confrontation.*

To stop these little monsters in their tracks, arm your meeting chair or organizer with some appropriate tools.

Gremlin 1: Bias

One way to deal with biases is to expose them to daylight. Since his days running Amazon in China and the UK, Doug Gurr has made it a discipline to insert pauses into deliberation processes. He was introduced to us by a mutual contact as "the smartest person I know", and yet he's more wary than most when it comes to the risks of biased thinking and the need to confront pre-existing beliefs and emotions.

Five or ten minutes into a job interview for a senior hire, for example, he tells interviewers to, "Ask yourself whether you feel like hiring this person or not. Surface your initial impression, and then spend the rest of the interview trying to disprove your hypothesis." By acknowledging your biases in this way, you're much more likely to be able to tackle them.

Gremlin 2: Groupthink

Groupthink requires a slightly different solution. London Business School Professor Sir Andrew Likierman, a long-time mentor of ours who researches judgement in organizations, suggests appointing a devil's advocate – someone who'll surface opposing views and probe for flaws in arguments.

---

* Don't get us wrong, we're all for diversity and for building a team that better represents society and brings varied viewpoints into the discussion. But it doesn't guarantee a great conversation on its own.

He brought this to life for us by sharing what he'd seen at German energy company RWE. In the 2010s it had to write off billions of euros of investments in conventional power, which were made against the current of an industry-wide transition to renewables. RWE determined that its executives had been excessively optimistic, that they fell victim to confirmation bias, and that junior employees didn't feel comfortable raising their objections. It has used devil's advocates in major meetings ever since.

"If you're worried there's going to be no discussion, ask someone to make the case against, even if it seems to be open and shut, just so those arguments are on the table," Likierman tells us.

This tactic was also used to great effect by President John F. Kennedy during the Cuban Missile Crisis.[24] Learning from his 1961 invasion of the Bay of Pigs, a decision which had proven disastrous, he ripped up his decision-making process two years later, just as the US entered into another geopolitical crisis.

In 1963, the US discovered Russian nuclear missile sites on Cuba. This was considered a direct provocation by its great rival at the peak of the Cold War. President Kennedy needed to respond quickly but he knew the wrong call could trigger nuclear war.

Not wanting to repeat his past mistakes on the island, he took a different approach to deciding how the US would react. Among other changes, he institutionalized dissent. He appointed two confidants as 'intellectual watchdogs' to find gaps or flaws in arguments, and prevent groupthink setting in. The fact we're here to tell the tale suggests this was a good move.

Gremlin 3: Fear of confrontation

However, requiring one person to disagree shouldn't absolve everyone else of the responsibility to speak out. Unfortunately, fear of confrontation can do just that.

We saw this in action at a board meeting in the US a few years ago. With its collegiate and meritocratic culture, the business was a champion of diversity which gave board seats to employee representatives.

As we walked into the boardroom, we were full of anticipation, eager to see this pioneering model in action. But it didn't live up to expectations. For most of the four-hour meeting, it was like someone had pressed the mute button for the employee board members. As the hours ticked by and the board worked diligently through its agenda, they did little more than murmur in agreement, or nod along, while the other board members dominated discussion. It took a quiet chat in a corridor, far from the boardroom, to reveal the truth – they were too nervous about the repercussions of speaking out to say what they really thought.

This fear of confrontation – and the silencing effect it produces – is particularly common among more junior employees, or in meetings with domineering personalities. To prevent it, you need to minimize the risk of conflict and lower the cost of disagreement.

You can even run an anonymous online poll to bring niggles out in the open without triggering discord.

Andrew White, an academic at Saïd Business School and CEO of leadership coaching firm transcend.space, builds his polls around two tried and tested questions that get groups talking: What is it that we're not talking about that we need to talk about? And what is it that we never resolve?

"It helps to shift the balance of power in the room, teasing out the issues that directors really want to tackle," he explains.

Following these three rules for better meetings will help to keep them centred on constructive, productive conversations that actually go somewhere useful. They will encourage people to use their brains, in the right way, by focusing on outcomes, not an ever-proliferating list of actions that turn them into busy fools.

But none of these new communication conventions will help if people don't follow them. So how can you make sure they do?

Chapter 6

Editors

How do you get everyone
to follow the rules?

"If I've told you once"

By August 9 1940, Winston Churchill had been the United Kingdom's Prime Minister for just three months. Those months had been long and painful – not just for Churchill but for his nation too.

France had fallen to Hitler, and Germany's destructive march across Europe showed no signs of slowing. The Luftwaffe had stepped up its deadly attacks on Britain from the skies. Despite Churchill's rousing speeches, the country's morale was at rock bottom. It felt to many like only a matter of time before German boots were on British soil.

On that summer's day, as the Battle of Britain raged, Churchill sat, frustrated, at his desk. Rather than grapple with military strategy or the mountain of letters and reports in his in-tray, he called in his secretary and dictated a memo.

As you might expect from one of history's great orators, a former war correspondent and a future winner of the Nobel Prize for Literature, Churchill chose his words carefully. And he got straight to the point.

"To do our work, we all have to read a mass of papers. Nearly all of them are far too long. This wastes time, while energy has to be spent in looking for the essential points.

"I ask my colleagues and their staffs to see to it that their reports are shorter."

Churchill went on (briefly, of course) to suggest succinct summaries at the beginning of full reports or occasionally in lieu of them, putting detailed analysis into appendices. He also asked civil servants to replace "officialese jargon" with shorter, more conversational phrasing.

"The saving in time will be great, while the discipline of setting out the real points concisely will prove an aid to clearer thinking," he concluded.

This now-famous note to his staff on the importance of clear, concise writing – titled 'Brevity' – was, in effect, a style guide. An attempt to codify and propagate the rules of good communication. Churchill was a very smart man, and this was a smart idea. At a time of national crisis, he couldn't afford for crucial information or ideas to be wasted.

So, what happened next?

Did the vast bureaucracy of the wartime British state suddenly transform into a powerhouse of crisp, clear expression? Was every report that graced the PM's desk thereafter all punch and no piffle?

To be brief, no.

A few months later, he must have felt a sense of déjà vu as he issued a fresh directive to his Secretaries of State.

"Forgive this cry of pain," he signed off as he implored them to follow his earlier advice. "The number and length of messages sent by a diplomatist are no measure of his efficiency," he advised.

Fast-forward 11 years, and déjà vu strikes yet again. Churchill, by then the elder statesman of British politics, had been back in Downing Street for just a few weeks. He sat at his desk and tapped out another pithy note. "In 1940 I called for brevity. Evidently I must do so again. I ask my colleagues to read what I wrote then ... and to make my wishes known to their staffs."[1]

He knew he sounded like a broken record. What he hadn't realized, however, was that a memo – or style guide – does not translate spontaneously into a culture of good communication, where everyone does it automatically. Even in the most hierarchical of organizations, and irrespective of the god-like status of the person writing it.

Most style guides gather dust on the company intranet somewhere near your HR policy documents and your compliance manual. Even if people do read yours (and we've read some great ones) they're hardly likely to walk around quoting it to each other. The chances are that most of what's contained will simply be forgotten. And besides, knowing what you ought to do is rarely sufficient as a method of behavioural change, as the history of public health campaigns has shown.[2] Everyone knows that smoking is bad for you, but people still do it.

So, to make consistent, quality communication stick, let's look elsewhere, and draw some inspiration from the world of journalism – and toilet seats.

Enforcing standards: Angry editors and *poka-yoke*

Twentieth-century newsrooms were noisy places, with telephones ringing and journalists thrashing at their keyboards amid the urgent, terse chorus of hacks talking over each other. Yet there was one sound that could bring it all to a brief, gasping silence: the dread shriek of the editor, who wants a word with you.

When a writer put up a sloppy paragraph or an incoherent structure, they got what we are assured by journalists was the technical term, 'a right old bollocking,' their egos bruised, their work returned to them lashed with red ink.

Of course, a great editor doesn't just berate – they guide, suggest, coach and remind people of the principles of their craft. We'd certainly all much rather be that kind of editor than the angry one.

But, to build an organization that can produce great communication consistently and at pace, you need both. You need to show people when they've missed the mark and then help them to find their way back to it.

The companies that do this best don't rely on style guides, role modelling and training, or employ armies of shrieking editors. Instead, they design methods that make it easy to apply the rules and help you spot when you're not.

The Japanese call this *poka-yoke*, or "mistake-proofing". It means designing a product or process in a way that makes it really hard to screw up.

The term was coined on Japan's manufacturing floor in the 1960s, and applications of *poka-yoke* can today be found in most modern manufacturing processes.

Take product assembly, for example. If a step in the process requires six screws, the worker on that part of the assembly line doesn't work their way through a huge box of screws. Instead, they're given screws in small containers, one per product, each with just six screws inside. If there's a screw left over, they know they've missed one out – and they can resolve their error before passing the product on to the next station.

Examples of *poka-yoke* can also be seen in everyday life. Automatic cars that won't start if they're not in 'park' or 'neutral', so you don't lurch forwards (or backwards). Filing cabinets that won't let you open more than one drawer at a time, to stop them falling over. Toilets that won't flush until you've shut the lid, so that you don't have to nag your partner to put the toilet seat down.

These days, modern software tools can be used in much the same way. Most of us are already using them to check our spelling and grammar, but you can take it further and use software to nudge your colleagues to adopt the communication principles that work, and to guide you back to the path when you stray off it.

We know this first-hand. After years of playing 'editor' ourselves with our clients' board papers – often being called in at 11pm to help draft (or redraft) a critical paper that a multi-million-dollar investment case depended on – we went looking for another way. Quite apart from valuing our sleep, we were ambitious and we knew it wasn't a scalable way to grow our business.

So, we raised some money and set to work building a software platform that could do the job for us – at any time of day, and for as many people who needed it at once, wherever they were in the world. Think of it as the love child of Microsoft Word's scribbly red line, Grammarly, Socrates and that newspaper editor (without the rage). Or, as the Japanese might say, the *poka-yoke* of great communication.

But whatever you do, and whatever tools you use, the objective should not be to police the letter of the law ('alert, alert: your semicolon use is in violation of paragraph 47, subsection 3 of the company style guide ...'). The aim should be to remind people of the spirit behind it – the core principles of good communication.

It's not a one-hit training programme or a memo. It's about making it easy, making it stick and building a capability that quickly starts to feel natural.

The rise of
the machines:
AI writers

But what of the rapid developments in generative AI that suggest that humans may not need to do the writing at all?

Certainly, AI promises to take on much more of the heavy lifting of crafting copy.

But even with this help, we will still need to be mindful of what good communication looks like. If you guide AI to use the old conventions, you'll just automate communication with all the old problems. For example, if you ask it to turn your first draft into something that sounds more technical and formal, it will. But what you'll get will be dry, heavy-going prose. And that (as you know) would be a mistake.

Guide the AI with better principles, and you'll get better outcomes. We've done this ourselves with our software platform, baking in AI to help our clients to spot passages of text that lack insight or that are hard to digest and reworking them at the click of a button.

At some point, AI may even make us redundant – making sense of data and other information for us, spitting out credible strategies and decisions in an instant.

But until we all enter the Matrix and outsource our thinking entirely, we need to take responsibility for our judgements. It isn't acceptable to shrug and say, "The computer told me to do it." Nor is it wise to expect AI to take half-baked ideas and make them taste good. Articulating what you think is part of getting that thinking and those judgements right.

This doesn't mean that AI won't be useful. We just need to see it, for the time being at least, as an assistant – something that can help us do it better – rather than a replacement. If it can help us articulate our ideas, making it easier for us to see flaws and implications, and suggesting ways of expressing it more clearly, then that's all for the better.

———————

Let's assume you do that, and everything else we've suggested to this point. You've given your team the tools for critical thinking and made it part of their day-to-day lives. You've shown them how to communicate that thinking with impact so that others act on it, and used nudges and perhaps AI to enhance those capabilities.

You've created, in effect, a squad of superheroes – individuals whose latent potential to reason and influence have been fully unleashed.

How do you make sure they use their powers wisely, so they're not just changing the wallpaper while the house is on fire? How do you make sure they don't clash, or pull your business in a thousand different directions at lightning pace?

Part III

Focus

**How will Part III help you build
collective intelligence?**

There's no point having a team of great
thinkers and brilliant communicators if their
efforts aren't pulling in the same direction;
the only thing you'll achieve is chaos. But too
much focus and you end up with tunnel vision.
In Part III, we'll show you how to achieve
single-minded focus while developing the
ability to pivot when you need to.

——— BOTTOM LINE UP FRONT ———

Chapter 7

Drumbeats

When does focus backfire?

All hands on deck

Storming a fortification is a dangerous way of spending your Tuesday afternoon. The defenders have a nasty habit of pelting you with rocks, arrows and the like.

Most ancient armies took the inevitable casualties as a cost of doing business. But the Roman army devised a way around it.

When Roman legionaries advanced under fire, they adopted a formation called the *testudo*, or turtle. They closed ranks and locked their shields together, at the front, on the sides and over their heads, forming a near impenetrable wall. Advancing in lockstep, they passed largely unscathed through the 'kill zone'. Victory followed, more often than not.

Such displays of unity were fundamental to Rome's rise as the greatest empire the Western world had seen. It wasn't just in the military.

As the Roman historian Vegetius observed, this was what gave them their competitive edge. "The Romans were less prolific than the Gauls, shorter than the Germans, weaker than the Spanish, not as rich or astute as the Africans, inferior to the Greeks in technology and in reason applied to human affairs. What they had was the ability to get organized."[1]

What Vegetius observed, and the Romans exploited to such dramatic effect, was the power of alignment, of everyone marching to the same beat. Without it, there is chaos: bickering, in-fighting, conflict and wasted effort.

With such a large population, huge distances between most provinces and Rome, and a prototype postal system (albeit one that wouldn't be matched for speed in Europe until the 19th century),[2] the Romans couldn't rely on micromanagement to conquer and then successfully govern.

Instead, emperors empowered local governors to deal flexibly with local issues.[3] These leaders had a shared focus – a belief in Rome itself – that cascaded through the administration from the palace and Senate downwards, helping to keep this vast organization cohesive for centuries.

Of course, these days – when we can speak to anyone, anywhere, anytime – it would be much easier to control an organization from the centre, even if it spanned time zones and oceans. And in a smaller organization, one you can get your arms around, even more so. Perhaps then, Rome isn't a model we can all learn from?

To understand just how powerful delegation still is and the crucial role focus plays in it, even at micro scale, let's fast forward 1,600 years, switch the Mediterranean for the Pacific Ocean and hop aboard the USS Santa Fe.

When it was launched in 1992, the Santa Fe was one of the US Navy's most advanced nuclear submarines.

But when David Marquet became its captain in 1999, it was the worst performer in the entire fleet. Morale among the 135 crew was abysmal, with a reenlistment rate of just 3% (the Navy average was around 20%).[4]

He didn't have a plan for turning it around. This was his first command, and it came out of the blue. When the Santa Fe order came, he'd just spent 12 months learning the ins and outs of an entirely different submarine, expecting that to be his first command. When fate intervened and he found himself climbing aboard the Santa Fe instead, he had none of the knowledge that would help him tell his crew how to improve.

That didn't stop him from trying though.

On one occasion, Marquet ordered a routine nuclear reactor shutdown drill. In these drills, speed is of the essence. While the reactor is down, the submarine is running on an electric back-up, but a 300-horsepower motor in a 6,000-ton submarine doesn't last long. The crew must race against time to get the reactor started again before the back-up runs out of juice.

To increase the sense of urgency and put the team under a little more pressure, he ordered the crew to increase the speed of the submarine to drain the battery even faster. "In every other submarine I've been on, there were two speeds to the electric motor. But unbeknownst to me, on the Santa Fe there's only one," Marquet said. The most experienced officer on deck passed on the order. "Aye, Captain. Increase speed."

"The sailor sitting at [the control] panel does nothing ... I said, 'Hey, what's going on?' He says 'Captain, on this ship, unlike your other ships, it's just one-speed motoring.' That was embarrassing."

The experienced officer knew about this too, so Marquet asked why he had passed on the order. "Because you told me to," came the reply. Like any good sailor, he had done what he had been trained to do: follow orders.

Marquet had spent his entire career learning how to get people to follow orders – winning trust, commanding respect, giving clear directives. In fact, his US Naval Academy textbook defined leadership as "directing the thoughts, plans, and actions of others ... so as to obtain and command their obedience."

But on the Santa Fe he realized that this was absurd, because he knew much less than the crew he was directing. "This was like a hammer blow to my head," he later recalled.

So, he flipped from trying to give better orders to giving no orders at all, instead talking in terms of intent.

For Marquet, rather than giving instructions ("Position the ship over there."), he would ask questions that communicated his intent and then let the crew make key decisions ("Our aim is to intercept the enemy, where do you think we should position the ship?"). For the crew, instead of seeking permission from Marquet ("Captain, request permission to submerge the ship."), they would tell him what they intended to do and why ("Captain, I intend to submerge the ship, it's safe to do it now and the best way to achieve our aim").

"It's a very small, nuanced change of language but it was hugely powerful because the psychological ownership now shifts to them. They need to discover the answer."

All very inspiring. Do you imagine it worked?

Sometime later, the Santa Fe was assigned to pick up a Navy SEAL team out at sea. The crew's aim was clear – to collect the SEALs and leave without being spotted.

These missions are always tense and fraught with danger, carried out in the middle of the night with no communication. To meet the SEALs, whose small rubber raiding craft would have just enough fuel to get them to the rendezvous point, the submarine would need to stop dead in the water and surface at just the right spot, at the right time.

As the clouds parted, the moon briefly illuminated the sleek hull of the Santa Fe as it came to the surface. While the submarine crew waited patiently for the SEALs to arrive, Marquet wandered the ship, checking in with the control room as they monitored the situation and their position. Everything seemed to be going fine – until an alarm sounded.

He raced back to the control room to find the ship had drifted out of position. If they didn't act quickly, they'd miss the SEALs. So, as he looked at the navigation display and the tension mounted, he slipped back into an old habit. He gave his first order in months. "The officer deck had already ordered ahead one-third. I'm looking at that and I say, 'No, back!'"

The quartermaster, one of the junior crew members in the room, immediately disagreed. "No, Captain, you're wrong," he said.

Marquet did a double take. He looked more closely at the monitors and realized the quartermaster was right "I'd gotten the direction of motion and the head of the submarine confused. We were actually pointing away. Ahead one-third was the perfect command."

Moments later – just as the Sante Fe got back into the correct position – the SEAL team arrived, and the mission was successfully completed.

Marquet was more than relieved. "If they had followed my order, we would have gotten out of position. We might've missed them." But even more satisfying was the realization that his changes were yielding fruit. "I could rest easy because now I had a crew that was trained for critical thinking, not compliance. My work was done."

Those changes proved potent – the Santa Fe became the top performing ship in the history of the US submarine fleet. Leading with intent, rather than orders, meant the crew took ownership for decisions. By asking questions rather than giving orders, Marquet had equipped them to think critically about the information in front of them. Concise and direct communication helped them cut through the noise. And, crucially, they shared a purpose and mission – crystal-clear focus – that helped them break down entrenched power dynamics and make the right call under pressure.

These are the essential foundations of an empowered organization and, with it, collective intelligence. People need both the tools to think and communicate well and a shared focus on the collective purpose and mission those tools are for.

But ...?

You know us so well. Focus is good. Indeed, giving people a common focus – a purpose, vision and mission that they believe in and can work toward – is a central feature of leadership. The sort of thing that *Leaders*, with a great big capital letter, do.

But too much focus isn't always a good thing. In fact, it can lead to some pretty major blind spots.

A cautionary tale comes from Silicon Valley, and famed internet browser Netscape. Some readers might not have heard of it, but that's the point.

In the late 1990s Netscape was a really big deal. The company's CEO was Jim Barksdale, a former CEO of AT&T Wireless and COO of FedEx. He took the company public in 1995 and quickly cornered 80% of the market.[5]

Barksdale, who hailed from Mississippi, had a "vast mental library of Southern homilies", and would regularly pepper conversations with his own brand of witty aphorisms. According to his former colleagues, one of his favourites was about focus: "The main thing is to make sure that the main thing stays the main thing."[6]

This presumably sounded sensible, coming from an eminent business leader like Barksdale. Unfortunately for Netscape, its 'main thing' was the wrong thing.

After a failed push into the enterprise market and subscription models, and with Microsoft offering superior service and a free-to-consumer product, the company reported its first quarterly and yearly losses in early 1998. The share price plunged, and it was acquired by AOL later that year. In 2007, the Netscape web browser was discontinued.

Barksdale was right to praise the virtues of focus but he missed an important point – that focus can easily turn into tunnel vision. If your flag is planted on the wrong hill, you'll end up in the wrong place. And, sometimes, you need to pivot to a new 'main thing.'

To thrive in a rapidly changing world, companies need both single-minded focus and the ability to change that focus when required.

How to stay focused but flexible

This is not easy. First of all, you have to realize that you're going in the wrong direction. Here a leader's individual strength – their single-mindedness and belief in what they are doing – can become a weakness, making it harder for them to accept that times have changed or that they were just wrong before.

To refocus, you need to ask yourself some big questions.

Are we still moving in the right direction? If we weren't already doing this, would we start doing it today? If you were a hungry young rival trying to disrupt our business, what would you do? Are we just reacting to what our customers say they want, rather than leading change in the market? How is today's success preventing tomorrow's?

These questions are too big and distracting for the day to day. Working *on* the business at this high level is easiest done when separated from working *in* the business. So, use rituals – carving space specifically and solely for organizational soul-searching, for example, in annual away days or retreats.

You could find ways of involving frontline employees to get their views. Hubert Joly, when he took over as CEO of beleaguered Best Buy in 2012, went undercover in stores for a week, to see and hear for himself what needed to change before launching a remarkably successful turnaround.[7]

And why not draw on the outside perspectives and experience of your board, and use your time with them to zoom out to the big picture?

However and whenever you do it, what really matters is that there is space for these questions to be asked, and that you are open to the possibility that you may need to change course.

But spotting that you need to pivot is only the first step – and it's the easiest one. The real challenge comes when you try to turn your 'new main thing' into everybody else's 'new main thing.'

Look at Nokia. In 2000, the Finnish giant was on top of the world, dominating the burgeoning mobile market with sleek, reliable and surprisingly resilient phones. *Snake*, its simple and highly addictive in-built game, with its "cellular serpent navigating the small, black-and-white screen," was a global phenomenon and had kick-started the mobile gaming industry.[8] Yet already its CEO Jorma Ollila recognized the need to change.

"In ten years' time I would like Nokia to be dubbed as the company that brought mobility and the internet together," he was quoted in *The Economist*.[9] Throughout the early 2000s, Ollila reiterated the importance of software, services, data and the internet to Nokia's continued success.

We all know what happened next. The iPhone came out in 2007, bringing mobility and the internet together in the way that Ollila had hoped to do. Nokia had only just stopped making 3310s. Its market share fell from 49% that year, according to Gartner, to 34% in 2010. By 2013, it had plummeted to just 3%, one of the most remarkable falls from grace in business history.[10]

The story is usually told as one of myopia, of a company that didn't see the need to change, but that isn't true. From Ollila's public statements in the early 2000s to the creation of Nokia Ventures as an incubator for new business models, Nokia's leadership had been trying to shift direction for years before its decline.

"We knew what was happening, but our mistake was not being able to turn that into action," Ollila later confirmed in his autobiography, *The Impossible Success*.[11]

"Maybe Nokia concentrated too much on cellular technologies. Maybe Nokia should've studied other wireless technologies ... but renewing the entire strategy of a corporation isn't easy when you've grown into a global market leader."

There are all sorts of reasons why a company like Nokia would have struggled to pivot. As Ollila indicated, its sheer size and bureaucratic inertia were a formidable obstacle. One employee later said the company's Chinese rivals could design and manufacture a new device in less time than Nokia took "to polish a PowerPoint presentation."[12]

Yet its employees were also undoubtedly focused on the things that had made the company successful – right until the point that those things ceased to make it successful, which was of course too late. The CEO repeatedly telling them that this needed to change was not enough to take their eyes off the old prize.

So, what is enough?

Chapter 8

Pivots

How do you get elephants to dance?

After 24 years in the news industry, including four years leading the Guardian Media Group, Dame Carolyn McCall decided it was time for a fresh start. Her new destination was the aviation sector, becoming CEO of European low-cost carrier easyJet in 2010.

She was a risky choice. Dismissed by her peers as a "media luvvie," she had never worked in the industry and was one of only a handful of women at the top of a FTSE 100 company (for most of her tenure, there would be more men called 'Dave' running FTSE 100 companies than women).[1] She might, to outsiders, have been considered a 'managed decline' sort of leader, given her background running newspapers – not the sort of person you'd bring in to restore a business to growth.

But growth was what easyJet needed. Oil was at well over $100 a barrel and consumer spending had yet to recover from the financial crisis. A volcano in Iceland had grounded European and transatlantic flights for weeks, and air traffic controllers all over Western Europe were striking for better pay and conditions. Against this challenging backdrop, easyJet's USP (low, low costs) had been eroded as competitors entered the space.

The previous management had responded by doubling down on their cost-cutting strategy, squeezing every drop out of the business to stay ahead. But there wasn't any fat left. The bones had been picked clean. Staff had to bring their own stationery to the office, which was in an aircraft hangar. Morale was dead on the ground, and customer satisfaction was right along with it.

McCall didn't need staff or customer surveys to tell her this. She walked the floors – in the HQ, airports and at 30,000 feet. She went up and down the aisles with a black bin bag in hand, collecting rubbish from passengers and chatting as she went. She talked with pilots and cabin crew over tea breaks and during layovers. And the conversations all pointed at the same problem: everyone was unhappy. Passengers because of poor service, the crew because of poor management. As she later wrote in a letter to pilots, "management lost sight of how big a difference having great people makes. It has taken its toll on how pilots feel about working for easyJet."[2]

She saw clearly that the two problems were connected. To make easyJet more competitive – to make it an airline that people wanted to fly with and work for – she needed to change the narrative. If she could lift the morale of her team, everything else would follow.

So, she flipped easyJet's priorities, from Profit-Customers-People to People-Customers-Profit.

Knowing that the best way to change the focus of an organization of independently minded people is to change the questions that they're asking, we worked with McCall to embed this new focus into the business. Implanting the following question into all board papers, KPI dashboards and management decks made it the number one question in the minds of managers: "How do our people feel, and what can we do better to support and enable them?"

By the time she left in 2017, she had doubled market share, increased revenues by 70% and profits by 162%.[3] Team, customer and shareholder satisfaction were transformed, because she got her people thinking about the right things. And it changed the rules of the game for the entire industry, prompting even Michael O'Leary, CEO of arch-rival Ryanair and airline sector offender-in-chief, to change his tune. Infamous for describing employees as less 'my most important asset' and more "lazy bastards,"[4] in 2016 he announced it was time for his airline to start "being nice to people."[5]

Most radical shifts in focus occur when a new leader, like McCall, takes over. They are motivated and able to break with the past, to question the wisdom of their predecessors' ideas. But you don't have to be fired and let a successor lead the change.

Let's learn from how McCall did it. The questions she put front and centre for her people were not the wonderings of a touchy-feely CEO, or a PR exercise. They directly determined the metrics, targets and incentives that drove the business.

By baking them into every decision paper and monthly management report, she made it difficult for her executives, and their teams, to lose focus. And she helped them link what they were doing with the new strategy and vision of the company.

She clearly and impactfully communicated that vision – one where happy crew led to happy customers, leading to better results – at every opportunity.

Marc Benioff, the founder of Salesforce, does something similar in a ritual he calls V2MOM, which he describes as critical to his company's ability to maintain alignment while growing to 80,000 employees.[6]

Each team, at every level of the company, asks five questions – Salesforce's version of a Question Driven Insight play – to help them understand where they are going and how they are going to get there:

1. Vision – what do you want to achieve?
2. Values – what's important to you?
3. Methods – how will you achieve it?
4. Obstacles – what could get in the way?
5. Measures – how will you know you've succeeded?

"What I like about the V2MOM is that it encourages creativity, change, and empowerment. Different team members can lead different methods, and they update the V2MOM as the year progresses. We think of the V2MOM as a living and breathing document," Benioff wrote in 2020.

To ensure alignment – and prevent 80,000 V2MOMs, and their authors, firing off in all directions – the starting point for the V2MOM cascade is Benioff and his senior team. Their V2MOMs hang from the same big picture goal. These documents then shape the V2MOMs of their direct reports, which inform their direct reports' V2MOMs, and so on through the organization. When the first drafts are done, managers check their teams' V2MOMs, making sure they're pointing in the same direction – and thus it goes right back up the chain, to the top.

This approach ensures the big picture goal is a common thread running through the process – one that is consistently applied, understood and supported by the plans of every individual and team, at every level.

It isn't just Benioff who appreciates the approach. His team, and their teams, are fans too. Phill Robinson, Salesforce's former chief marketing officer, told us it was popular not just because it created alignment, but because "it helped you get the best out of people." At every level, "people could critically appraise the plans and then decide independently, for themselves, how they were going to respond. They felt they were able to contribute."

Robinson has used the V2MOM model in all the companies he's run since leaving Salesforce. At IRIS, the software business that Robinson led through several rounds of private equity ownership, the approach helped employees to connect with its mission in a way they hadn't before, and it led to much deeper engagement. "For the first time, because the V2MOM made such a clear link between our mission and the activities we were all engaged in, people could see that we were doing something purposeful and meaningful," he recalled.

Rituals built around QDI plays, like the V2MOM, allow a common understanding of the company's focus to cascade through the business – at all levels, and any scale. And, as easyJet shows, you can change the questions, or bring new ones in, when you need to change that focus.

It's a journey we're on ourselves, as we write this. For years our focus was on our domestic market but more recently we've started to build the foundations for international expansion and voice our international ambitions. But it's quite a mindset shift, and it requires more than just a few speeches or copy-all emails.

We've updated the questions that our teams ask themselves in their QD1 plays, and this is changing the conversation. Adding in the question "How does this support our international goal?" is encouraging us to think about what we might need to do differently to be as successful around the world. It's helping our people to apply their own intellectual energies in the same direction and the right direction.

––––––––––

Asking questions drives thinking. Great communication turns thinking into action. And focus ensures all of this is directed toward common goals, however big your team or organization.

It's *really* inconvenient, then, that history is littered with examples of people doing all of this and getting nowhere... It sticks a pin in our thesis.

Or does it?

When it all goes wrong

What do you want to do
with your power?

Chicago was bustling that Christmas Eve. The 1954 holiday season was in full swing and the city's residents, wrapped up tight against the biting wind, zipped around the city making their final preparations for the following day's festivities.

As the sun set on a house in Oak Park, a Chicago suburb, final preparations of another kind were underway.

Charles, a doctor at the local college, perched uncomfortably on the arm of the sofa as his eyes scanned the room. The house was packed. Bumping elbows with the man on his left and trying not to lean too heavily on the woman sitting on his right, he put his hands in his lap and took a deep breath.

Charles didn't need his medical degree to know he was full of adrenaline. He could feel his pulse racing and beads of sweat forming on his brow.

That evening, the Supreme Being was going to send a flood to devastate large swathes of North America and Europe. Chicago was squarely in its path. In a few hours' time, the house he was sitting in would be under 10 feet of water.

But Charles wasn't scared. Quite the opposite – it was hope and excitement that had sent the adrenaline coursing through his veins. His friend Dorothy had been chosen by The Guardians to lead a small, select group of devout followers, Charles included, to safety. A flying saucer would be sent to rescue them from the impending apocalypse at 6pm sharp.

By 6.20pm it was clear something was wrong. The Guardians were late. Charles looked nervously at Dorothy, but her face gave nothing away. Maybe she knew something he didn't?

As the minutes ticked by, Charles' excitement turned to fear. Would they be saved, or would they meet a watery grave along with the non-believers? Members of the group fired increasingly panicked questions at the group's leader. Charles' heart rate continued to climb.

Just as the tension looked like it might boil over, Dorothy received an urgent message from The Guardians. Because of their unswerving devotion, God had decided to spare the Earth. There was no need to send the flying saucer. Everyone cheered.

'That was close, but thank goodness we kept the faith,' Charles thought to himself as he made his way home wearing a satisfied smile.

The next day he returned to Dorothy's house. The believers set out joyously, with their faith renewed, to share the good news – that, thanks to them and their devotion, everyone was safe.[1]

––––––––––––––

You may assume that you and your colleagues are rather shrewder than these members of an obscure 1950s doomsday cult. But belief perseverance – the persistence of a belief despite new and compelling evidence to the contrary – is so powerful and pervasive that it has been described by philosopher Ferdinand Schiller as a "fundamental law of nature."

This was the fourth time in just over a week that The Guardians had promised the end of the Earth, arranged to save Dorothy and her followers, and then failed to show. Did this shake their faith in any way? Not a bit. Their faith was as strong as ever.

Belief perseverance emerges from the discomfort we experience when confronted by information that requires us to change our minds. And we've seen it already in this book, under various guises. Sometimes it manifests through ego, other times through complacency or hubris, or social conformity, or a seemingly inbuilt resistance to change. However it appears, it is the great enemy of new ideas, questioning, innovation, reason, agility and adaptation.

Harry Markopolos found out the hard way just how widespread it is. In the year 2000, he was an equity portfolio manager for a Boston-based hedge fund, Rampart Investment Management. He'd spent 17 years as a part-time reservist in the National Guard. And he was a brilliant mathematician with a liking for brown suits.

His colleague Frank Casey, then head of marketing at the firm, heard about a hedge fund that was delivering consistently strong returns – and hoovering up a lot of business. Could Markopolos work out how, and backwards engineer them an approach that would deliver the same results? "Harry, if you can do this for me, we can make a lot of money," Casey pleaded.

The hedge fund in question was Bernard L. Madoff Investment Securities. Its founder, Bernie Madoff, wasn't shy. In fact, he was rather a big deal. He ran one of Wall Street's largest market makers, chaired the Nasdaq board and sat on advisory committees for the US Securities and Exchange Commission (SEC).

But, just out of view and under the radar, he was running a highly secretive hedge fund business notable for its exclusive clientele. And he was making them a lot of money.

Through a customer of Madoff's, Markopolos was able to get his hands on the numbers and he set about trying to figure it out. How was Madoff able to do something no one else could, and beat the market so consistently? The task was right up his street.

"It took me five minutes to know it was a fraud ... it took me another almost four hours of mathematical modelling to *prove* that it was a fraud," he later told *60 Minutes*.[2]

So Markopolos did what any other law-abiding citizen would do. He went to the authorities.

The SEC ignored him.

He wrote to them again the following year, and again in 2005, 2007 and spring 2008. His 2005 submission was particularly damning. Markopolos produced a crisp, 21-page memo called simply "The world's biggest hedge fund is a fraud," in which he made the case against the deeply respected Madoff with forensic precision and persuasive, pithy prose.[3]

He showed that it was a Ponzi scheme that never even traded.

He showed that its results were statistically impossible.

He showed its strategy required buying more options on the exchange than existed at the time.

His analyses fell on deaf ears. A few cursory, bungled investigations came and went, but nothing happened.

Journalists also tried to jolt the SEC into action. After one article in *MARhedge* claimed Madoff's investment advisory business was unregistered – a violation of federal regulations – there was a brief moment where the regulator looked set to take action.[4] A Washington SEC official knew Madoff, so she cut to the chase by giving him a call.

As recounted by H. David Kotz, who later led the official investigation into the SEC's enquiries, the conversation went like this:

> **SEC official:** "Hi Bernie, we're gonna do an exam, we're going to have some questions about your hedge fund."
> **Madoff:** "I don't have a hedge fund."
> **SEC official:** "Oh, I didn't think so."
> **Madoff:** "OK." [*puts the phone down*][5]

It took the financial crisis to finally bring Madoff and his fraud to light – and only then because he ran out of cash to keep the Ponzi scheme going.

What went wrong?

You can't fault the incisive quality of Markopolos's thinking, nor indeed the clarity or impact with which he communicated it, nor even the focus and persistence with which he pursued his cause over those eight years. He displayed everything we've advocated for, but it still failed.

It failed because belief perseverance won. The regulators – who were far from stupid – didn't want to believe they had been wrong about Madoff for all those years. They couldn't believe he was a crook.

Belief perseverance is a mighty foe. And many of those we now revere as the most brilliant thinkers of their age suffered brutally at the hands of it.

At the start of this book, we introduced Socrates, the "father of critical thinking" and waxed lyrical about his questioning skills as the root of critical and creative thought. What we failed to mention was that the more his questions challenged the status quo, the more people he upset; the Athenians eventually did him in with a hemlock cup.

If you're more into science than ancient philosophy, spare a thought for Galileo. Some 2,000 years after Socrates' death, the Italian astronomer argued convincingly that the Earth moves around the Sun and not the other way around, flying in the face of scientific consensus at the time. He wrote his thesis in the form of a witty dialogue – a series of questions and answers exchanged between three people – which helped to make it accessible and compelling. He also made himself guilty of heresy in the process. The Roman Inquisition sentenced him to life imprisonment and his book was banned for the next 200 years.

Throw in the t(r)owel

This fly in the ointment has two key implications for you as a leader trying to nurture collective intelligence.

Firstly, it means you can't just stop when *some* people are thinking and communicating well. A great insight will go nowhere if no one is listening, or if those who do listen refuse to change their minds, as Markopolos discovered.

Collective intelligence won't work in pockets. There may be flashes of brilliance, but they can fizzle out. It will not be enough for a chain reaction. Critical thinking, great communication and a shared focus on what matters must be the lifeblood of your entire organization.

Secondly, even if you achieve system wide collective intelligence, you can't rest on your laurels. Over time we revert to type and your carefully constructed culture can unravel – even if it has delivered results. It can be all too easy for once-questioning minds to start believing in the brilliance of their own ideas or insights, rather than in the process that created them.

Like a garden, collective intelligence requires maintenance. You can't will the plants in your garden to grow the way you want, but if you – as leader, or head gardener – nurture the ecosystem, sowing seeds, watering, nourishing and protecting, then it will flourish.

Belief perseverance is the Japanese knotweed of cognitive processes, so how do you rip it out when you find it in your garden? Or, better still, defend against it so it doesn't take root in the first place?

Overcoming belief perseverance

It's a scourge that famed investor Ray Dalio has been solving since the early days of his fund, Bridgewater.

For well over a decade Bridgewater has been the world's largest hedge fund.[6] Dalio is a billionaire nineteen times over and one of the richest people in the world.[7] But Bridgewater's journey to world domination wasn't a smooth one.

Early on, Dalio learned just how painful belief perseverance can be. Helpfully for us, he also figured out how to defend himself, and his business, against it.

In 1982, the then 33-year-old investor predicted a crisis. US banks were over-exposed to Latin American countries that were rapidly becoming incapable of repaying their debts. Sure enough, Mexico defaulted in August that year. Dalio's personal stock rocketed. He found himself on the cover of magazines and testifying before Congress as an expert on the crisis.

Then it all went south. Or rather, it didn't. Dalio believed that the banking crisis would cause a depression worse than in the 1930s and buoyed by his recent success, he bet the shop on it. But it turned out that August 1982 was the bottom of the stock market, not the beginning of a total collapse. He'd called it wrong.

Dalio's clients deserted him, and he had to let everyone in his team go. "I was so broke I had to borrow $4,000 from my dad," he later told *The Knowledge Project* podcast.[8]

"It was a terrible experience, but it turned out to be one of the most valuable experiences in my life because it changed my approach to decision-making. I went from thinking 'I'm right' to asking myself 'How do I know I'm right?'"

From that very low point, Bridgewater's rise was meteoric. After successfully preparing for and weathering the 2008-9 financial crisis, it became the largest hedge fund in the world in 2011.[9]

Dalio attributes this success to a culture of radical open-mindedness, transparency, and thoughtful disagreement.

"The greatest tragedy of mankind is to hold ideas in our heads that are wrong, that [we] are attached to and don't stress test. It is so easy to take those ideas, and in a meritocratic way put them out there to stress test and raise that probability of being right," Dalio explained.

His continued insistence on doing so, on propagating and nurturing a culture where everyone asks the question "How do I know I'm right?" is a prime example of a leader 'gardening' – weeding out belief perseverance wherever it pops up and ensuring that the principles of collective intelligence are universally applied.

Over to you

We've spent much of the 30,000 or so words of this book encouraging you not to hoard power, but to share it. But we can't ignore that, as a leader, you have considerably more power than the average person on the street. We want you to feel powerful and we want you to use that power well.

So, what do you want to do with your power?

In recent years, a rising swell of political and economic disempowerment has turned into a tidal wave of disillusion – and it's starting to impact society and threaten democracy itself.

Those who aren't lucky enough to belong to 'the club' – sitting in positions of power, and amassing wealth, resources, and privilege – feel increasingly powerless. They feel trapped in a system that wasn't set up with their interests in mind, in which the door to a better life has been locked shut with the key thrown away.

Rising inequality. Flatlining productivity. Popularism. All signs of this growing sense of 'us versus them.' All indicators of the rising disengagement, dislocation and distrust felt by ever larger portions of the population. You don't have to go far on social media or spend much time eavesdropping on conversations in cafés to see or hear it. Why trust business leaders, politicians and the media when they are only interested in serving their own interests? If the system isn't working for you, why not put your trust in someone who pledges to burn it down for you?

You're reading the same headlines as everyone else. But the difference is that, as a business leader, you're not a passive agent in all of this. You have power. And you can use that power to do something about it.

You have the power to change the system. You decide how your business works, and how your business works with its people.

You can create the conditions for more and better thinking. You can rip up the old communication rule-book and replace it with something more powerful. And you can change the questions your people are asking of themselves and others, to focus their thinking on the things that matter most.

You have the power to involve all of your people as active agents within that system and to take away the constraints that stifle their creativity and productivity. To help them live up to their potential and be more of who they were meant to be.

By building collective intelligence – giving people the freedom to make decisions and supporting them with the skills and tools to discharge their responsibilities well – you don't just help them perform better, you give them their voice back too.

You've no way of knowing what they might say when you do. But we bet you're curious to find out.

Further reading

The 'Collective Intelligence' book site
Resources to help you build collective intelligence
in your organization, including QDI plays,
interactive tools and checklists
www.collectiveintelligence-book.com

Charlotte Woffindin's blog, 'Doc Bar Raiser'
Great tips for business writing from a former
Amazon executive and 'Writing Bar Raiser'
www.docbarraiser.com

Dr Lani Watson's website
Dr Watson's research on questions, and tools to test
your questioning skills
www.philosophyofquestions.com

***The Pyramid Principle: Logic in Writing and
Thinking*, Barbara Minto**
Barbara Minto's classic guide to rigorous thinking
and writing changed the game for both of us,
in different ways

The Economist Style Guide

We've always admired The Economist's writing style; this guide is a useful reference for anyone looking to write more clearly and concisely

Monzo's 'tone of voice' guide

A summary of Monzo's communication principles, this is an irreverent guide to writing like a human
www.monzo.com/tone-of-voice/

The Dialogues of Plato

A masterclass in questioning from Socrates' student Plato

Endnotes

UPSIDE-DOWN

1. Emma Priestley, Board Intelligence, "60 seconds with…
    John Timpson CBE," 12 June 2013
    https://www.boardintelligence.com/blog/60-seconds-with-john-timpson-cbe
    (accessed 24 August 2023)

2. Kristian Brunt-Seymour, "The power of 'upside-down management'",
    HR Magazine, 14 June 2017

3. Business Sale Report Insights, "Upside Down Management –
    will more business leaders operate like Timpson post-pandemic?"
    https://www.business-sale.com/insights/for-buyers/upside-down-
    management-will-more-business-leaders-operate-like-timpson-
    postpandemic-221372 (accessed 24 August 2023)

4. Zameena Mejia, "Steve Jobs Almost Prevented the Apple iPhone
    from Being Invented," *CNBC*, 12 September 2017
    https://www.cnbc.com/2017/09/12/why-steve-jobs-almost-prevented-the-
    apple-iphone-from-being-invented.html (accessed 24 August 2023)

5. Brian McCullough, "The History of the iPhone on its
    10th Anniversary," *Internet History Podcast*, 6 January 2017
    https://www.internethistorypodcast.com/2017/01/the-history-of-the-
    iphone/ (accessed 24 August 2023)

6. Anupreeta Das, "Warren Buffet's Heirs Bet on Apple",
    The Wall Street Journal, 16 May 2016
    https://www.wsj.com/articles/buffetts-berkshire-takes-1-billion-position-
    in-apple-1463400389 (accessed 24 August 2023)

CHAPTER 1

1. Dr Robert Cade, *The Piss Prophets*, Cade Museum
    Originally hosted at https://www.cademuseum.org/
    *uploads/2/5/7/2/25721946/chapters_10-11_2c_gatorade_2c_the_piss_*
    prophets.pdf (accessed 1 June 2023)

2. Gilbert Rogin, "The Bottle And The Babe," *Sports Illustrated*,
    01 July 1968
    https://vault.si.com/vault/1968/07/01/the-bottle-and-the-babe
    (accessed 1 June 2023)

3. Joe Kays and Arline Phillips-Han, "Gatorade: The Idea that Launched
    an Industry," University of Florida
    https://research.ufl.edu/publications/explore/v08n1/gatorade.html
    (accessed 1 June 2023)

4. Statista, "Sales of the Leading Sports Drink Mixes Brands in the
    United States in 2021"
    https://www.statista.com/statistics/326655/us-sales-of-the-leading-sport-drink-mixes-brands/ (accessed 1 June 2023)

5. Thomas Rogers, "Why Won't You Answer Me?"
    (interview with Peter Harris, Harvard Graduate School of Education),
    Salon, 20 May 2012
    https://www.salon.com/2012/05/20/why_wont_you_answer_me/
    (accessed 1 June 2023)

6. Wendy Berliner, "'Schools are Killing Curiosity': Why We Need
    to Stop Telling Children to Shut Up and Learn," *The Guardian*,
    (referencing Susan Engel, *The Hungry Mind*, 2015), 28 January 2020
    https://www.theguardian.com/education/2020/jan/28/schools-killing-curiosity-learn (accessed 1 June 2023)

7   George Land, "The Failure of Success," *TEDxTucson*, 29 October 2013
    https://www.youtube.com/watch?v=EtCD4aEHr4A&t=37s (accessed 1
    June 2023)

8. Claudia H. Deutsch, "At Kodak, Some Old Things are New
    Again," *The New York Times*, 2 May 2008 https://www.nytimes.
    com/2008/05/02/technology/02kodak.html (accessed 1 June 2023)

9. Behnam Tabrizi, "How Microsoft Became Innovative Again",
    Harvard Business Review, 20 February 2023
    https://hbr.org/2023/02/how-microsoft-became-innovative-again
    (accessed 6 September 2023)

10. Greg Shaw, Jill Tracie Nichols and Satya Nadella, *Hit Refresh:
    The Quest to Rediscover Microsoft's Soul and Imagine a Better Future
    for Everyone*, 2017

11. Sal Khan, "Education Reimagined," *IBM Think*, 2018
    https://www.ibm.com/support/pages/education-reimagined-sal-khan-ibm-think2018 (accessed 1 June 2023)

CHAPTER 2

1. "Rob Whiteman Leaves Home Office for New Chief Executive Role," *gov.uk*, 27 June 2013
   https://www.gov.uk/government/news/rob-whiteman-leaves-home-office-for-new-chief-executive-role (accessed 1 June 2023)

2. Richard Ford, "Immigration Backlog of 500,000 Cases Will Take 40 Years to Clear, Complain MPs," *The Times*, 13 July 2013
   https://www.thetimes.co.uk/article/immigration-backlog-of-500-000-cases-will-take-40-years-to-clear-complain-mps-s8ks2fw7kcs (accessed 1 June 2023)

3. *Daily Mail*, various articles, 2012
   https://www.dailymail.co.uk/news/article-2102895/Immigrant-crimewave-warning-Foreign-nationals-accused-QUARTER-crimes-London.html (accessed 1 June 2023)
   https://www.dailymail.co.uk/news/article-2145556/One-tip-minutes-illegal-immigrants-database.html (accessed 1 June 2023)

4. John Vine, Independent Chief Inspector of the UK Border Agency, "An Investigation into Border Security Checks," February 2012
   https://assets.publishing.service.gov.uk/government/uploads/system/uploads/attachment_data/file/546243/Report-of-the-UKBA-ICI-Report_2012-02-20.pdf (accessed 1 June 2023)

5. Mazher Mahmood, "My Man Can Fix Immigration Papers to Keep You in Britain," *The Times*, 13 November 2013
   https://www.thetimes.co.uk/article/my-man-can-fix-immigration-papers-to-keep-you-in-britain-2sg26wzxvws (accessed 1 June 2023)

6. *Bill and Ted's Excellent Adventure*, Orion Pictures, 1989

7. Bent Flyvbjerg and Dan Gardner, "How Frank Gehry Delivers On Time and On Budget," *Harvard Business Review Magazine*, January-February 2023
   https://hbr.org/2023/01/how-frank-gehry-delivers-on-time-and-on-budget (accessed 1 June 2023)

8. Peter Aspden, "Interview: Frank Gehry," *Financial Times*, 22 November 2013
   https://www.ft.com/content/1c87963c-51cb-11e3-8c42-00144feabdc0 (accessed 1 June 2023)

9. Catherine Slessor, "Guggenheim Museum in Bilbao, Spain by Frank O. Gehry & Associates," *Architectural Review*, 12 December 1997
   https://www.architectural-review.com/buildings/guggenheim-museum-in-bilbao-spain-by-frank-o-gehry-associates (accessed 1 June 2023)

10. Bent Flyvbjerg and Dan Gardner, *How Big Things Get Done*, 2023

11. "The Combat Estimate," *Wikipedia*
    https://en.wikipedia.org/wiki/Combat_Estimate (accessed 1 June 2023)

12. Albert Read, *The Imagination Muscle*, 2023

CHAPTER 3

1. Jeffrey K. Liker, *The Toyota Way: 14 Management Principles from the World's Greatest Manufacturer*, 2004

2. G. Frederick Thompson, "Fordism, Post-Fordism, and the Flexible System of Production," Center for Digital Discourse and Culture, Virginia Tech
   https://www.cddc.vt.edu/digitalfordism/fordism_materials/thompson.htm (accessed 1 June 2023)

3. Opex Learning, "TPS – The History of the Toyota Production System"
   https://opexlearning.com/resources/tps-the-history-of-the-toyota-production-system/23618/ (accessed 4 July 2023)

4. i) "Eiji Toyoda," *Wikipedia*
   https://en.wikipedia.org/wiki/Eiji_Toyoda (accessed 1 June 2023)

   ii) Market cap in USD on 30 August 2013 taken from Companies Market Cap
   https://companiesmarketcap.com/ (accessed 1 June 2023)

5. Francesca Gino and Michael I. Norton, "Why Rituals Work,"
   Scientific American, 14 May 2013
   https://www.scientificamerican.com/article/why-rituals-work/ (accessed 1 June 2023)

6. David L. Goodstein and Judith R. Goodstein, *Feynman's Lost Lecture*, 1996

CHAPTER 4

1. Larry Van Dyne, with John Pekkanen and Daniel Rapoport, "A False Feeling of Security: The Inside Story of the Crash of Air Florida's Flight 90," *The Washingtonian*, October 1982
   https://www.washingtonian.com/wp-content/uploads/2022/01/Air-Florida-Wash-1982-copy.pdf (accessed 1 June 2023)

2. Del Quentin Wilber, "A crash's improbable impact," *NBC News*, 12 January 2007
   https://www.nbcnews.com/id/wbna16591533 (accessed 16 August 2023)

3. Chad Plenge, The Center for Junior Officers, "Copilot Leadership: What We Can Learn from the Airline Industry" *https://juniorofficer.army.mil/copilot-leadership/* (accessed 16 August 2023)

4. Tait Elder, "New Ventures: Lessons from Xerox and IBM," *Harvard Business Review Magazine*, July-August 1989 *https://hbr.org/1989/07/new-ventures-lessons-from-xerox-and-ibm* (accessed 1 June 2023)

5. Robert C. Alexander and Douglas K. Smith, *Fumbling the Future: How Xerox Invented, Then Ignored, the First Personal Computer*, 1999

6. "Better.com Boss Uses Zoom Call to Lay Off 900 Employees," *The National News*, 6 December 2021 *https://www.youtube.com/watch?v=9nBQGWF4Cpg* (accessed 1 June 2023)

7. Boris Groysberg and Michael Slind, "The Silent Killer of Big Companies," *Harvard Business Review*, 25 October 2012 *https://hbr.org/2012/10/the-silent-killer-of-big-companies* (accessed 1 June 2023)

CHAPTER 5

1. Adam Gale, "Why Amazon Banned PowerPoint," *Management Today*, 15 July 2020 *https://www.managementtoday.co.uk/why-amazon-banned-powerpoint/leadership-lessons/article/1689543* (accessed 1 June 2023)

2. Jeff Bezos, *Twitter*, 13 May 2022 *https://twitter.com/JeffBezos/status/1525188353704050690* (accessed 1 June 2023)

3. Dr Chris Atherton, "Visual Attention: A Psychologist's Perspective," School of Psychology, University of Central Lancashire *https://www.slideshare.net/CJAtherton/chris-atherton-at-tcuk09* (accessed 1 June 2023)

4. Jeff Bezos' Letter to Shareholders, 2017 *https://www.sec.gov/Archives/edgar/data/1018724/000119312518121161/d456916dex991.htm* (accessed 1 June 2023)

5. Taylor Locke, "Jeff Bezos: This Is the 'Smartest Thing We Ever Did' at Amazon," *CNBC*, 14 October 2019 *https://www.cnbc.com/2019/10/14/jeff-bezos-this-is-the-smartest-thing-we-ever-did-at-amazon.html* (accessed 1 June 2023)

6. Elisabeth Bumiller, "We Have Met the Enemy and He Is PowerPoint,"
The New York Times, 26 April 2010
https://www.nytimes.com/2010/04/27/world/27powerpoint.html
(accessed 1 June 2023)

7. R. C. Victorino, "How Stripe Built a Writing Culture," *Slab*,
2 September 2020
https://slab.com/blog/stripe-writing-culture/ (accessed 1 June 2023)

8. Gregory Ciotti, "To Create a Culture of Writing at Your Company,
Start by Providing Incentive," *Think Growth*, 15 May 2017
https://thinkgrowth.org/to-create-a-culture-of-writing-at-your-company-start-by-providing-incentive-c393e777d80f (accessed 1 June 2023)

9. Linda Lai and Audun Farbrot, "What Makes You Click? The Effect
of Question Headlines on Readership in Computer-mediated
Communication," *Social Influence*, Volume 9, 2014 – Issue 4,
25 October 2013
https://www.tandfonline.com/doi/full/10.1080/15534510.2013.847859
(accessed 1 June 2023)

10. *Friends (Season 10, Episode 5)*, "The One Where Rachel's Sister
Babysits," 2003

11. Rudolf Flesch, "How to Write Plain English," 1979
https://pages.stern.nyu.edu/~wstarbuc/Writing/Flesch.htm
(accessed 6 July 2023)

12. Edwin L. Battistella, "Reading, Writing and Readability–Appreciating
Rudolph Flesch," 6 October 2019
https://blog.oup.com/2019/10/reading-writing-and-readability-appreciating-rudolph-flesch/ (accessed 1 June 2023)

13. Daniel M. Oppenheimer, "Consequences of Erudite Vernacular
Utilized Irrespective of Necessity: Problems with Using Long Words
Needlessly," *Applied Cognitive Psychology*, (20: 139-156, 2006),
31 October 2005
https://www.affiliateresources.org/wp-content/uploads/2022/01/ConsequencesErudite.pdf (accessed 1 June 2023)

14. Tsuyoshi Okuhara et al. "Influence of High Versus Low
Readability Level of Written Health Information on Self-efficacy:
A Randomized Controlled Study of the Processing Fluency Effect,"
Health Psychology Open, 12 February 2020
https://journals.sagepub.com/doi/10.1177/2055102920905627
(accessed 1 June 2023)

15. Mary Beard, "What I Wish I Had Known When I First Started Out as a Writer," *Sunday Times* Charlotte Aitken Young Writer of the Year Award, *http://www.youngwriteraward.com/mary-beard-what-i-wish-i-had-known/* (accessed 1 June 2023)

16. "Our Tone of Voice," *Monzo* *https://monzo.com/tone-of-voice/* (accessed 1 June 2023)

17. Clive Humby's speech at the 2006 Association of National Advertisers Senior Marketer's Summit, Kellogg School, as reported by Michael Palmer *https://ana.blogs.com/maestros/2006/11/data_is_the_new.html* (accessed 31 July 2023)

18. Dr Steve Rogelberg (University of North Carolina) and Otter research, "'One-third of Meetings Are Unnecessary, Costing Companies Millions (and No One is Happy About it)," 26 September 2022 *https://otter.ai/blog/one-third-of-meetings-are-unnecessary-costing-companies-millions-and-no-one-is-happy-about-it* (accessed 1 June 2023)

19. Leslie A. Perlow, Constance Noonan Hadley and Eunice Eun, "Stop the Meeting Madness," *Harvard Business Review Magazine*, July-August 2017 *https://hbr.org/2017/07/stop-the-meeting-madness* (accessed 1 June 2023)

20. Matthew Boyle, "Shopify Tells Employees to Just Say No to Meetings," *Bloomberg*, 3 January 2023 *https://www.bnnbloomberg.ca/shopify-tells-employees-to-just-say-no-to-meetings-1.1865187* (accessed 1 June 2023)

21. Jon Bergman, "Flipped Learning," 1 July 2014 *https://www.youtube.com/watch?v=BHM5ypLCiBA* (accessed 1 June 2023)

22. Valerie Strauss and Jay Mathews, "The Flip: Turning a Classroom Upside Down," *The Washington Post*, 3 June 2012 *https://www.washingtonpost.com/local/education/the-flip-turning-a-classroom-upside-down/2012/06/03/gJQAYk55BV_story.html* (accessed 1 June 2023)

23. Jonathan Bergman and Aaron Sams, *Flip Your Classroom: Reach Every Student in Every Class Every Day, 2012* and *Flipped Learning: Gateway to Student Engagement, 2014*

24. Patricia Roehling and Carrie Bredow, "Flipped Learning: What is It, and When is It Effective?", *The Brookings Institution*, 28 September 2021 *https://www.brookings.edu/blog/brown-center-chalkboard/2021/09/28/flipped-learning-what-is-it-and-when-is-it-effective/* (accessed 1 June 2023)

25. Michael A. Roberto, *Why Great Leaders Don't Take Yes for an Answer: Managing for Conflict and Consensus*, 2005

CHAPTER 6

1.   i)   "Winston Churchill," *Wikipedia*
         https://en.wikipedia.org/wiki/Winston_Churchill (accessed 1 June 2023)

     ii) "The Blitz," *Britannica*
         https://www.britannica.com/event/the-Blitz (accessed 1 June 2023)

     iii) "Churchill's Call for Brevity," *The National Archives*, 17 October 2013
         https://blog.nationalarchives.gov.uk/churchills-call-for-brevity/
         (accessed 1 June 2023)

     iv) Jim Edwards, "This Memo from Winston Churchill on
         'Brevity' Is All You Need to Improve Your Writing," *Business
         Insider*, 26 May 2017
         *https://www.businessinsider.com/memo-winston-churchill-on-
         brevity-improve-writing-2017-5* (accessed 1 June 2023)

2.   Katherine R. Arlinghaus, "Advocating for Behavior Change With
     Education," *American Journal of Lifestyle Medicine*, December 2017
     *https://www.researchgate.net/publication/321707370_Advocating_for_
     Behavior_Change_With_Education* (accessed 1 June 2023)

CHAPTER 7

1.   Lester C. Thurow, *The Future of Capitalism: How Today's Economic
     Forces Shape Tomorrow's World*, 1997

2.   "Message-relay Systems of the Ancient World," *Britannica*
     https://www.britannica.com/topic/postal-system/History#ref367055
     (accessed 1 June 2023)

3.   "The Roman Republic," *Khan Academy*
     *https://www.khanacademy.org/humanities/world-history/ancient-
     medieval/roman-empire/a/roman-republic* (accessed 1 June 2023)

4.   i)   Mark Gordon, "Marquet's Navy," *Business Observer Florida*, 9
         November 2012
         *https://www.businessobserverfl.com/news/2012/nov/09/marquets-
         navy/* (accessed 1 June 2023)

     ii) Simon Sinek, *Leaders Eat Last: Why Some Teams Pull Together and
         Others Don't*, 2013

iii) Talks at Google, "Turn the Ship Around, L. David Marquet,"
22 August 2017
https://www.youtube.com/watch?v=IzJL8zX3EVk
(accessed 1 June 2023)

iv) David Marquet, *TEDxScottAFB*, 21 June 2012
https://www.youtube.com/watch?v=DLRH5J_93LQ
(accessed 1 June 2023)

v) David Marquet, *Leadership Nudges*, 17 May 2014
https://www.youtube.com/watch?v=pYKH2uSax8U&t=445s
(accessed 1 June 2023)

5. "Barksdale, Jim," *Encyclopedia.com*
https://www.encyclopedia.com/economics/encyclopedias-almanacs-transcripts-and-maps/barksdale-jim (accessed 1 June 2023)

6. Greg Miller, "Netscape's Navigator," *Los Angeles Times*, 8 February 1998
https://www.latimes.com/archives/la-xpm-1998-feb-08-fi-16789-story.html (accessed 1 June 2023)

7. Adam Gale, "What I Learned Leading One of America's Great Turnarounds," *Management Today*, 4 May 2021
https://www.managementtoday.co.uk/what-i-learned-leading-one-americas-great-turnarounds/leadership-lessons/article/1714461 (accessed 1 June 2023)

8. Ayla Angelos, "The History of Snake: How the Nokia Game Defined a New Era for the Mobile Industry," *It's Nice That*, 23 February 2021
https://www.itsnicethat.com/features/taneli-armanto-the-history-of-snake-design-legacies-230221 (accessed 1 June 2023)

9. "A Finnish fable," *The Economist*, 12 October 2000
https://www.economist.com/business-special/2000/10/12/a-finnish-fable (accessed 1 June 2023)

10. Dave Lee, "Nokia: The Rise and Fall of a Mobile Giant," *BBC*, 3 September 2013
https://www.bbc.co.uk/news/technology-23947212 (accessed 1 June 2023)

11. Jorma Ollila, *Mahdoton menestys (The Impossible Success)*, 2016

12. Charles Arthur, "Nokia's Chief Executive to Staff: 'We Are Standing on a Burning Platform,'" *The Guardian*, 9 February 2011
https://www.theguardian.com/technology/blog/2011/feb/09/nokia-burning-platform-memo-elop (accessed 1 June 2023)

CHAPTER 8

1. "Carolyn McCall Wins Over Critics in 7 Years at easyJet," *Financial Times*, 17 July 2017 *https://www.ft.com/content/985b8a82-6b05-11e7-bfeb-33fe0c5b7eaa* (accessed 1 June 2023)

2. Dave Woods, "Easyjet Moves to Address Pilot Lifestyle and Industrial Relations," *HR Magazine*, 3 June 2011 *https://www.hrmagazine.co.uk/content/news/easyjet-moves-to-address-pilot-lifestyle-and-industrial-relations* (accessed 1 June 2023)

3. Arun Kakar, "Carolyn McCall's 3 Biggest Achievements as easyJet CEO," *Management Today*, 21 November 2017 *https://www.managementtoday.co.uk/carolyn-mccalls-3-biggest-achievements-easyjet-ceo/women-in-business/article/1450836* (accessed 1 June 2023)

4. Michael Hogan, "Michael O'Leary's 33 Daftest Quotes," *The Guardian*, 8 November 2013 *https://www.theguardian.com/business/shortcuts/2013/nov/08/michael-o-leary-33-daftest-quotes* (accessed 1 June 2023)

5. Simon Gwynn, "EasyJet's Carolyn McCall: When You've Done Something Wrong, Apologise," *Campaign*, 26 April 2017 *https://www.campaignlive.co.uk/article/easyjets-carolyn-mccall-when-youve-done-something-wrong-apologise/1431750* (accessed 1 June 2023)

6. Marc Benioff, "Create Strategic Company Alignment With a V2MOM," *salesforce.com*, 1 May 2020 *https://www.salesforce.com/blog/how-to-create-alignment-within-your-company/* (accessed 1 June 2023)

WHEN IT ALL GOES WRONG

1. i) Frank R. FioRito, "The Seekers of Cuyler Avenue," *Oak Park River Forest Museum*, 24 December 1954 *https://oprfmuseum.org/this-month-in-history/seekers-cuyler-avenue* (accessed 1 June 2023)

   ii) Leon Festinger, Henry Riecken and Stanley Schachter, *When Prophecy Fails: A Social and Psychological Study of a Modern Group That Predicted the Destruction of the World*, 1956

iii) Julie Beck, "The Christmas the Aliens Didn't Come," *The Atlantic*, 18 December 2015 *https://www.theatlantic.com/health/archive/2015/12/the-christmas-the-aliens-didnt-come/421122/* (accessed 1 June 2023)

iv) Whet Moser, "Apocalypse Oak Park: Dorothy Martin, the Chicagoan Who Predicted the End of the World and Inspired the Theory of Cognitive Dissonance," *Chicago Magazine*, 20 May 2011 *https://www.chicagomag.com/city-life/may-2011/dorothy-martin-the-chicagoan-who-predicted-the-end-of-the-world-and-inspired-the-theory-of-cognitive-dissonance/* (accessed 1 June 2023)

2. "The Man Who Figured Out Madoff's Ponzi Scheme," *60 Minutes*, 2009 *https://www.youtube.com/watch?v=3wUJesUik5A* (accessed 1 June 2023)

3. Harry Markopolos, "The World's Largest Hedge Fund is a Fraud," 25 October 2005 *https://www.sec.gov/news/studies/2009/oig-509/exhibit-0268.pdf* (accessed 1 June 2023)

4. Michael Ocrant, "Madoff Tops Charts; Skeptics Ask How," *MAR/Hedge (No. 89)*, May 2001 *https://nakedshorts.typepad.com/files/madoff.pdf* (accessed 1 June 2023)

5. *Madoff: The Monster of Wall Street*, Netflix, 2023

6. Avery Coop, "Ranked: The World's 20 Biggest Hedge Funds," *Visual Capitalist*, 7 December 2022 *https://www.visualcapitalist.com/worlds-20-biggest-hedge-funds-2022/* (accessed 1 June 2023)

7. "The World's Real-Time Billionaires," *Forbes* *https://www.forbes.com/real-time-billionaires/#36e6b5fd3d78* (accessed 1 June 2023)

8. "Ray Dalio: Principles for a Life Well Lived," *Knowledge Project Podcast*, 27 September 2022 *https://www.youtube.com/watch?v=pl2_6KP2HpY&t=704s* (accessed 1 June 2023)

9. Imogen Rose-Smith, "The Top Hedge Funds Of 2011," *Business Insider*, 12 May 2011 *https://www.businessinsider.com/the-top-10-hedge-funds-of-2011-2011-5?* (accessed 1 June 2023)

Acknowledgements

There are two names on the front cover of this book, but we couldn't have written a book about collective intelligence on our own. We owe our deepest thanks to all those who made it possible.

To the inspiring group of business leaders, academics and writers we interviewed for our research: Guillaume Alvarez, Silvana Bonello, Sir George Buckley, Sir Mick Davis, Rob Enslin, Doug Gurr, Ann Hiatt, Andrew Hill, Professor Sir Andrew Likierman, Pete Miller, Phill Robinson, Oliver Shah, Paul Stobart, Dr Lani Watson, Rob Whiteman, and Charlotte Woffindin.

To everyone who has supported Board Intelligence, including our employees and clients past and present. Particular thanks go to Dame Carolyn McCall and Chris Kennedy who, as CEO and CFO of easyJet, gave us a major break in the early days.

To the team at LID for their advice, challenge and patience throughout the publishing process.

And lastly, to our colleagues Megan Pantelides and Adam Gale, who helped us to get our thinking straight and find the words to do it justice. We couldn't have done this without you.

About the authors

Jennifer Sundberg
Jennifer is co-CEO of Board Intelligence.

Jennifer began her career in strategy consulting and is a serial entrepreneur, having founded her first business in her early 20s. She holds an MA from Cambridge University and The Judge Business School.

Jennifer is a regular speaker at conferences and events and has written regular columns for *Management Today*. She has played a vocal role in shaping governance best practice in the UK and internationally, and has won numerous awards including EY Entrepreneur of the Year for London and *The Times* Young Business Woman of the Year.

Pippa Begg
Pippa is co-CEO of Board Intelligence.

Pippa started her career in financial services, working for HM Treasury and leading global investment manager Russell Investments, after graduating from Cambridge University with an MA in Natural Sciences.

Pippa is a guest lecturer at Henley Business School and a regular speaker at conferences and events. She has played a vocal role in shaping governance best practice in the UK and internationally and has won numerous awards including EY Entrepreneur of the Year for London and *Management Today*'s '35 women under 35.'

Board Intelligence

Board Intelligence is a mission-led technology firm that transforms boards and leadership teams into a powerful driver of performance and a force for good. Today, Board Intelligence supports more than 3,000 organizations and 40,000 directors globally, from Fortune 500 and FTSE 100 corporates to government departments and charities.